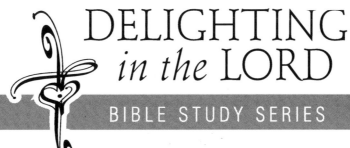

DELIGHTING IN A LIFE LIVED FOR GOD

A Study on the Book of 1 Peter

by Stacy Davis and Brenda Harris

A Ministry of Calvary Chapel Chester Springs

Delighting in a Life Lived for God
A Study on the Book of 1 Peter
Part of the Delighting in the Lord Bible Study Series

© Copyright 2020
Calvary Chapel Chester Springs
PO Box 595, Eagle, PA 19480

ISBN 9781661695125

Series Cover Design: Melissa Bereda
Cover Photo: Stacy Davis, Sea of Galilee

Printed in the United States of America

"The one thing I ask of the Lord - the thing I seek most - is to live in the house of the Lord all the days of my life, delighting in the Lord's perfections and meditating in his temple." Psalm 27:4

DELIGHTING
in the LORD
BIBLE STUDY SERIES

CONTENTS

DELIGHTING IN A LIFE LIVED FOR GOD

A Study on the Book of 1 Peter

CONTENTS

DELIGHTING IN A LIFE LIVED FOR GOD

A Study on the Book of 1 Peter

"But may the God of all grace, who called us to
His eternal glory by Christ Jesus,
after you have suffered a while, perfect,
establish, strengthen, and settle you."
1 Peter 5:10

ACKNOWLEDGMENTS

"There are diversities of gifts, but the same Spirit.
There are differences of ministries, but the same Lord.
And there are diversities of activities but it is the same God who works all in all.
But the manifestation of the Spirit is given to each one for the profit of all."
1 Corinthians 12:4-7

Many people with different gifts have come together for the common purpose of sharing God's Word (Matthew 28:19-20). This study is the product of those people and their gifts working together by God's grace. We are so thankful for each person and the role they fill.

Pastor Chris Swansen - Theological Editor, Calvary Chapel Chester Springs
Pastor Steven Dorr - Pastoral Support, Calvary Chapel Chester Springs
Carinna LaRocco - Copy Editor
Joan Purdy - Copy Editor
Melissa Bereda - Graphic Designer
Lynn Jensen - Office Support
Chris Good - Photographer

A huge thank you as well to the families that allow us to use their second homes for writing getaways.

Additionally, we could not fulfill this calling without the love and support of our husbands and children. From the time God called us to write women's Bible studies, we have considered the call "our reasonable act of service" (Romans 12:1) to Him. Our families and those involved in the DITL ministry join us in this calling. We pray these studies will be used by God to draw many deeper into His Word to the heart of God so that lives and relationships will be transformed by His great power and grace.

With love in Christ,
Stacy and Brenda
Delighting in the Lord Ministry

ABOUT THE DELIGHTING IN THE LORD MINISTRY

In 2006 Stacy and Brenda were separately called by the Lord to begin ministering to women. Stacy began teaching a Thursday morning Bible study for women at her home church, Calvary Chapel Chester Springs. Each Thursday the ladies met for a Bible teaching and a small group discussion. Meanwhile, Brenda began a traveling teaching ministry called Life Applications Ministries. Their paths would not cross for two more years. What they did not know was God would form a partnership to fulfill both of their callings, together, in a way neither of them would have foreseen. God was laying the groundwork for the Delighting in the Lord Ministry.

In 2008 Stacy asked Brenda to join the Thursday Bible study as a small group leader. The small group leaders helped with the teaching load, and this became the first year that Stacy and Brenda ministered together.

For the next two years, Brenda and Stacy taught the women who gathered on Thursday mornings using Bible study materials from other Calvary Chapel churches and authors. In 2010 Stacy was diagnosed with invasive breast cancer, and Brenda became more hands-on in the women's ministry. It was during that year that God planted the writing seeds in Stacy's and Brenda's hearts. Sensing the Lord's direction to study the book of Matthew the following year, Brenda and Stacy searched for a women's Bible study on Matthew. They found nothing that covered the whole book in a verse-by-verse format with an emphasis on life applications. As Stacy prayed seeking God's direction, God continued speaking to her heart, telling her to "write the study." With much fear and trepidation, Stacy shared this with Brenda who also began diligently praying for God's direction. As Brenda sought the Lord, He gave her the READ format vision, and then He gave them both Psalm 27:4 which became their ministry verse and foundation:

"The one thing I ask of the Lord, the thing I seek most, is to live in the house of the Lord all the days of my life, *delighting in the Lord's* perfections, and meditating in His temple." (NLT)

After much prayer and with the faith to believe that since God called them He would equip them, the *Delighting in the Lord Bible Study Series* was birthed that year.

2011 was spent studying and writing "Delighting in the King," a women's Bible study on the book of Matthew. God brought many key people to support the work including Pastor Chris Swansen, who read every page of the study for Biblical accuracy. Seeing the need, God also touched the hearts of two women, Carinna LaRocco and Joan Purdy, who became our copy editors. They review our written words and make sure our studies are without writing errors. He also provided a graphic designer, Melissa Bereda. She has designed all of the logos, covers, and interior pages. Each person God brought to partner with Stacy and Brenda in this ministry has answered God's call on their life to use their gifts for God's glory.

The next year, upon suggestion from the ladies attending the Thursday morning study, the teaching sessions were video recorded, and the church began putting all the materials online. These teaching videos are available at www.delightinginthelord.com. Since then, God has used Brenda and Stacy to teach His Word, both in written and spoken form, to the women who gather together on Thursday mornings as well as to women online, individuals, and those in other study groups and churches.

What began as a simple "Yes, God" became a ministry that teaches God's Word to women, drawing out His truths and life applications. They are simply two women who love Jesus with their whole hearts and lives. They have experienced the power of the cross in their own lives and want to tell others of the saving power and grace of Jesus, so others can live a life of peace and joy in the midst of life's chaos. Even more, so that others can live with hope, knowing their eternal home with Jesus awaits. They are humbled hearing testimonies of God's transforming work of the Holy Spirit as women have used these studies to delve into God's Word.

DELIGHTING
in the LORD
BIBLE STUDY SERIES

ADDITIONAL STUDIES IN THE
DELIGHTING IN THE LORD BIBLE STUDY SERIES

Each verse-by-verse study is inductive and deductive with life application emphasis following the **READ** format: **Receiving** God's word, **Experiencing** God's word, **Acting** on God's word, and **Delighting** in God's word.

Delighting in God, His Righteousness and Perfect Plan: Romans

Delighting in Being a Child of God: 1, 2 & 3 John

Delighting in God's Will and His Provision: Jonah & Nahum

Delighting in the Redeemer, a Love Story: Ruth

Delighting in God's Heart: A study on the Life of David through
1 & 2 Samuel and the Psalms

Delighting in The Holy Spirit: Acts

Delighting in Being a Woman of God: Esther

Delighting in a Life of Triumph: A study on the life of Joseph
from Genesis 37–50 (Amazon)

Delighting in God's Wisdom: Proverbs (Amazon)

Delighting in the King of Kings: Matthew Volume 1: Chapters 1–9 (Amazon)

Delighting in the King of Kings: Matthew Volume 2: Chapters 10–20 (Amazon)

Delighting in the King of Kings: Matthew Volume 3: Chapters 21–28 (Amazon)

For additional information about the ministry, please go to:
www.delightinginthelord.com.
All studies and videos of corresponding teachings are available at:
www.cc-chestersprings.com/DITL.
A few of the studies are available for purchase on Amazon.com (see above).

DELIGHTING in the LORD
BIBLE STUDY SERIES

ABOUT THE AUTHORS

STACY DAVIS has been teaching women God's Word for over 15 years. She has learned many Biblical truths through difficult trials. Beginning at the age of three with her mother's brain aneurism, to the death of her fourth son and through invasive breast cancer, Stacy's faith has been tried and tested many times over. Her life gives testimony to God's redeeming and transforming power. Stacy teaches the truths of God's Word with passion, desiring to share with all women how to go through everyday struggles victoriously in Jesus Christ. She lives in PA with her husband, Barclay. They have six children.

BRENDA HARRIS's background in education, along with her many years as a classroom teacher, was foundational for the plans God had for her to serve Him. In 2006, she transitioned away from instructing young people how to read literature and began teaching women how they can have a closer walk with the Lord through reading and studying their Bible. She is an enthusiastic teacher who loves a great visual to help demonstrate practical ways to apply God's Word to real life. Brenda lives in PA with her husband, Michael, and their two children.

DELIGHTING
in the LORD
BIBLE STUDY SERIES

INTRODUCTION

DELIGHTING IN A LIFE LIVED FOR GOD

A Study on the Book of 1 Peter

Peter appears on the scene for the first time in John 1:35-42 as his brother, Andrew, is introducing Peter to Jesus. It was at this time that the two brothers chose to follow Him. Perhaps the introduction went something like this:

"Simon! Simon! Where are you?"
"Andrew, stop shouting. I'm over here by the fishing nets! What's wrong?"
"Nothing is wrong; actually, everything is finally, perfectly, right! We have found the Messiah! Come with me Simon and meet the Christ!"
"What are you talking about, Andrew? How do you know it is Him?"
"Just come with me, and you will see for yourself!"

Simon Peter likely met Jesus sometime around 27 A.D. through his brother Andrew. This introduction would change his life forever. Over the course of the next forty years, he would leave his career of fishing and become a fisher of men because of God's calling on his life. Peter was one of the disciples closest to Jesus. Scripture identifies Peter with three different names: Simon, Cephas, and Peter. Two of these names Jesus gave him personally: Cephas (John 1:42) and Peter (Matthew 16:18). These names seem to point almost to a progression in his walk with God. Simon means "hearing," Cephas means "a stone," and Peter means "a rock."

For three years Peter would be a disciple of Jesus and follow Him everywhere. At times he would be brazen and impetuous, while at other times fearful; he would even deny knowing Christ. But over those three years, he had a front row seat to some of the most incredible miracles as well as Christ's transfiguration, resurrection, and ascension back to heaven. Those years were tumultuous for Peter and certainly could be considered his training ground for what Christ would accomplish through him once Christ's time on earth was finished.

Whatever Peter may have lacked prior to the day of Pentecost, he certainly made up for once the Holy Spirit resided within him. Acts 2:14-41 records Peter's first public sermon, and it was so Spirit filled and powerful that 3,000 souls were added to the church that day. Peter healed many sick and lame people. He restored Tabitha to life. Further, he would help open the way for the Gentiles to be part of the church as God shows no partiality (Acts 10:34), desiring all to be saved.

Despite all the amazing ways God used Peter in the early church, he would also suffer greatly for the cause of Christ. He was placed in prison many times and understood the concept of persecution and suffering. It is from this vantage point, many believe, Peter wrote 1 and 2 Peter. By the time he wrote these letters, he would be close to the end of his life. He was likely in prison awaiting his death when he wrote them. And yet, these letters are filled with profound hope, encouragement, and theology. Peter may have been once considered an "unlearned fisherman," but after having spent time with Jesus for three years and later empowered by the Holy Spirit, his letters are anything but simpleminded.

AUTHOR
The author is Simon Peter, Son of Jonah.

AUDIENCE
Peter is writing to the "Elect Pilgrims" (1 Peter 1:1), likely a group of both Jews and Gentiles living in Asia Minor, which is modern day Turkey.

DATE
The book of 1 Peter was likely written between 62-64 A.D. before the burning of Rome in July 64 A.D.

WEEKLY WRITTEN LESSONS
This study on 1 Peter has been broken into ten weeks. Each week there is only one "day" of homework, which means that you will only go through the R.E.A.D. format once a week. There will be one or two "Experience" sections for each week. In this section you will read the verses and answer questions from the text. After you go through the text, you will move on to the application section called "Acting on God's Word." Here you will apply what you've learned to your own life. This is such a necessary step so be sure to take the time to consider how God is speaking to your heart and life. The last section is your time to reflect and delight in God and what He has taught you. We will ask you to end with a verse God spoke to your heart that week. This would be a great verse to memorize.

You may choose to do your homework in one sitting or in many; it is totally up to you. You should allow 60-90 minutes to complete the whole week's study. We highly encourage you to spend the time in God's Word while answering these questions and digging into the text for yourself. You will find that your time investment will be given back to you deeply for your spiritual growth.

FORMAT: "READ" THE BIBLE

*The format for this study follows the acronym **READ**: Read the Bible.*

RECEIVING God's Word

1. **Open in Prayer:** Before reading God's word, you need to prepare your heart to receive from Him what He has for you.
   - During this time of prayer, confess any sin that may be present in your life.
   - Ask God to open "the eyes of your heart" (Eph 1:18) so you can hear from Him what He wants to communicate to you.
   - Thank Him in advance for what He will do!
2. **Receiving:** Read the scripture text given.

EXPERIENCING God's Word

This is where you will dive into the Bible and the daily chapter/verses. You'll be answering questions that lead you through the text by first observing the details and then focusing on the connections within the text to the bigger picture. At other times, you may be investigating other verses from the whole counsel of God and then drawing some Biblical conclusions from what you have read. There may be several "experiences" drawn from the text.

ACTING on God's Word

In this part of the study you will be applying these verses to your life. We read in Hebrews 4:12 that God's word is "living and powerful, and sharper than any two-edged sword, piercing even to the division of soul and spirit, and of joints and marrow, and is a discerner of the thoughts and intents of the heart." Therefore, as you are studying, God will be speaking to your heart and life. We will be encouraging you to look at applications, but God may have other things He is speaking to your heart. We pray you hear directly from Him. As you listen to the Lord speak to your heart, may He show you what steps He desires you take as you walk out your faith in Him.

DELIGHTING in God's Word

In this final section you will reflect upon what you have learned and offer up your praise and thanksgiving to the Lord. As you close out your daily time, may you truly find that He is the delight of your heart! He fills like no other and nothing else can. And as you "delight yourself in the LORD" He will give you the desires of your heart (Psalm 37:4), because after studying His word, your desires and His should be the same. Through your time in God's word, may you grow more and more into His image. You will be asked to record a verse (or as many as you want!) that stood out to you from the text and then memorize it if you so desire.

"The one thing I ask of the Lord - the thing I seek most - is to live in the house of the Lord all the days of my life, delighting in the Lord's perfections and meditating in his temple." Psalm 27:4

DELIGHTING IN MY SALVATION

If you have never accepted Jesus Christ as your Savior but desire to take that step of faith, all you need to do is:

Recognize that God loves you!
"For God so loved the world that He gave His only begotten Son, that whoever believes in Him should not perish but have everlasting life." (John 3:16)

"But God demonstrates His own love toward us, in that while we were still sinners, Christ died for us." (Romans 5:8)

Admit you are a sinner.
"For all have sinned and fall short of the glory of God." (Romans 3:23)

"As it is written: 'There is none righteous, no, not one;' " (Romans 3:10)

Recognize Jesus Christ as being God's only remedy for sin.
"For the wages of sin is death, but the gift of God is eternal life in Christ Jesus our Lord." (Romans 6:23)

"But as many as received Him, to them He gave the right to become children of God, to those who believe in His name:" (John 1:12)

"For I delivered to you first of all that which I also received: that Christ died for our sins according to the Scriptures, and that He was buried, and that He rose again the third day according to the Scriptures." (1 Corinthians 15:3-4)

Receive Jesus Christ as your personal Savior!
"If you confess with your mouth the Lord Jesus and believe in your heart that God has raised Him from the dead, you will be saved." (Romans 10:9)

Prayer is simply "talking with God." Right now, go to God in prayer and ask Christ to be your Savior. You might pray something like this:

"Lord Jesus, I need You. I confess that I am a sinner and that You paid the penalty for my sin through Your death on the cross. I believe that You died for my sins and were raised from the dead. I ask You to come into my heart, take control of my life, and make me the kind of person that You want me to be. Thank You for coming into my life as You promised." Amen.

If you have prayed to accept Christ as your Savior, please tell someone today! Share this exciting news with a close Christian friend, your small group leader, or your pastor. They will be thrilled to encourage you in your faith and your decision to follow Jesus!

WEEK 1

A PILGRIM'S PERSPECTIVE

1 Peter 1: 1-12

For Peter and the other disciples, it was a day much like the others they'd spent with Jesus – unpredictable. Since being called to follow Him, each day they saw new towns, new people, new miracles, and often new healings. Their days were filled with traveling the dusty roads around Jerusalem and encountering many hurting people. Jesus always seemed to press into the hurt, the suffering, and the questions; taking time to go beyond the apparent need to the places of the heart. Having traveled with Jesus for over a year, what was predictable were the deep lessons of faith that came with each new encounter.

Today would be no different. Leaving a Samaritan village behind them, the disciples walked with Jesus to the next village. With the sun rising in the sky above and rocky ground underneath their feet, they traveled together. Many wanted to know this man called Jesus and often followed Him as they journeyed. As they were pulling away from the crowd, there came a voice saying, "Lord, I will follow you wherever You go." Standing before them was a man eager to join them. Jesus didn't miss a step. The disciples intently listened as Jesus told this man that those who choose to follow Him are travelers. Their footing isn't in this world. "Foxes have holes, and birds of the air have nests, but the Son of Man has nowhere to lay His head." (Luke 9:58)

This wasn't the answer the man expected. He didn't know what to say. In the silence, another chimed in and pledged his devotion to Jesus and then another did the same. But Jesus soon saw their devotion was conditional. The needs of life called for their attention and devotion first. The world's grip was just too tight.

Peter took it all in as Jesus looked at the men and spoke. Here came the faith lesson. "No one having put his hand to the plow, and looking back, is fit for the kingdom of God." (Luke 9:62) Those men left the group that had gathered around Jesus. The cost was too high to follow Him.

I believe the seeds of discipleship were planted deep in Peter's heart that day. Jesus would build on that foundation soon after as He sent seventy men out to local cities to preach of the kingdom of God. In the sending, Jesus told them to take no money, no sandals, no knapsack. Stay where you are welcomed and eat what you are given.

There was kingdom work that needed to be done and a world that needed to hear about Jesus. Shortly before, Jesus gave these same instructions to His twelve disciples as He sent them out too. The pieces were coming together. The message was being made clear: Hand to the plow, kingdom work, kingdom focus, travel light, always look forward.

We are travelers, not dwellers. This world is not the final destination. Heaven awaits those who have chosen to follow Jesus. As Peter opens his letter to Christian believers, it is from this perspective he will encourage those he calls "pilgrims."

A pilgrim is a traveler; one who journeys a long distance to a sacred place with a destination in view. Despite the time it takes to get there, the pilgrim keeps traveling knowing that destination will one day be reached.

Having been dispersed from Jerusalem out into the surrounding areas, these Christian pilgrims are also traveling through foreign lands. They are weighed down with all kinds of trials on their travels; those things that can test faith and tell us to give up. But Peter is quick to remind them, as he reminds us, this world is not our home. A heavenly inheritance awaits us.

In Christ we are all pilgrims in this world. We are but traveling through a foreign land, on a sacred journey, to a sacred place far off in the future. Yet, as far off as it may seem, we know it's close and getting closer each day. Peter tells us because of Jesus Christ, we can be hopeful travelers. We should be expectant travelers, filled with faith and joy, keeping God's promise of heaven always in front of us.

Oh, how the flesh wants to dig its footing into this world and call it "home." The enemy is always tempting us with the allures of this world and making our mark in it; bigger houses, fancy cars, topnotch diplomas, titles after our names. He tries to make us live like permanent residents, not pilgrims. It is a battle we have to fight. I, Stacy, fight it alongside you. But even in the battle, Peter tells us in 1 Peter 1:5 we are "kept" or guarded by the power of God through faith. God, holding us tightly throughout our pilgrimage, asks us only to believe in Him and to be ready to receive all the blessings that await us at the end of the journey.

RECEIVING God's Word

Open in Prayer
Read 1 Peter 1:1-12

E EXPERIENCING God's Word

Experience 1: 1 Peter 1:1-2

1. In verse 1 our author is introduced. Peter is writing to the dispersed Jewish believers throughout Asia Minor who are not living in their homeland. How does Peter address the recipients of this letter?

2. Verse 2 gives the words and phrases: *election, sanctification, obedience,* and *sprinkling of the blood.* These are defining words for the believer who has put their faith in Jesus Christ and has been washed by His blood for salvation. If you have never received Jesus Christ as your Lord and Savior, please turn to the Introduction pages and read the "Delighting in your Salvation" section. If you have already put your trust in Jesus, then these words define you. Let's read more about what God's Word says about them. Read the verses below and note what you learn.

ELECTION (INDIVIDUAL'S CHOSEN TO ETERNAL LIFE BY GOD'S FOREORDAINING LOVE AND THE SOVEREIGN GRACE OF GOD):

1 Peter 1:20

Ephesians 1:4

SANCTIFICATION (THE SPIRIT'S SETTING APART OF THE BELIEVER AS CONSECRATED TO GOD):

2 Thessalonians 2:13

1 Thessalonians 5:23

OBEDIENCE (THE RESULT OR END AIM WHICH FLOWS FROM FAITH IN GOD AND LOVE FOR HIM):

Romans 1:5

Romans 16:26

SPRINKLING OF THE BLOOD (DAILY CLEANSING FROM SIN):

Romans 3:25

Romans 5:9

1 John 1:9

3. Now let's take these four concepts and see how the trinity fulfills them. Fill in the blanks below with the trinity (God, the **Father,** Jesus, the **Son** and the **Holy Spirit** – see verse 2 where they are mentioned together in one verse)

_____ elected us.

_____ saved us and offers us spiritual cleansing.

_____ sanctifies us and helps us to be obedient.

"We have been chosen by the Father, purchased by the Son, and set apart by the Spirit. It takes all Three if there is to be a true experience of salvation. As far as God the Father is concerned, I was saved when He chose me in Christ before the foundation of the world. As far as the Son is concerned, I was saved when He died for me on the cross. But as far as the Spirit is concerned, I was saved one night in May 1945 when I heard the Gospel and received Christ. Then it all came together. But it took all Three Persons of the Godhead to bring me to salvation. If we separate these ministries we will either deny divine sovereignty or human responsibility, and that would lead to heresy." (W. Wiersbe, *Be Hopeful*, p. 31)

4. Explain how election, sanctification, obedience to the faith and spiritual cleansing are all examples of God's grace to us.

   a. You can't have peace with God until you experience His grace. How does the peace of God come through these four areas? Don't miss the last word in verse 2. It's a gem!

Experience 2: 1 Peter 1:3-5

1. Peter begins verse 3 with words of praise and worship thanking God for the gift of salvation through God's mercy. What are the promises we are given in verses 3-5?

    a. Are these promises for us today or for the future? Explain.

2. In verse 3 Peter uses the phrase "begotten us again." This phrase is another way to say we are saved. When speaking to Nicodemus in John 3:3 & 5, Jesus said, "You must be born of water and spirit in order to enter the Kingdom of God." Read 2 Corinthians 5:17. After we have been born of the Spirit, what are we in Christ and what is the importance of this?

3. Describe what it means to have a *"living hope."* (vs. 3)

4. Fill in the following blanks from 1 Peter 1:5.

    "We are _____ by the power of God through _____ for _____ ready to be revealed in the last time."

a. The word *kept* means "to be shielded or guarded as by a military guard." How does the power of God do this through our faith? How long does this protection last?

Experience 3: 1 Peter 1:6-12

1. In 1 Peter 1:6 we are told we can greatly rejoice despite difficult circumstances. The first two words in verse 6 are "In this" which points us to the preceding verses. From what you just learned and according to this verse, how can we rejoice in various trials?

2. Read 1 Peter 1:6-7. We are told we experience various trials so that the genuineness of our faith can be tested. Describe what genuine faith looks like. Why does faith need to be tried?

a. According to 1 Peter 1:7, there is a specific way God tests our faith which can happen through fire. In Isaiah 48:10 and Malachi 3:3, God uses the analogy of being a goldsmith who refines precious metals. He is the refiner, and our faith is like gold or silver. A refiner must sit in front of a hot furnace while a lump of gold is being heated to high temperatures so that the impurities can be pulled out of the gold. When this happens, the gold now holds value. The refiner does not pull the gold out until he sees his reflection in the gold. Apply this to the life of a believer.

3. Read 1 Peter 1:8-9. We see the word *believe* used here which means "to trust or put our confidence in someone." In this case, in a God we have not seen. If we are believing in God through a difficult trial, then what should be our attitude?

    a. Read 2 Corinthians 4:16-5:1. What are we told about our afflictions and eternity?

> We must keep in mind that all God plans and performs here is preparation for what He has in store for us in heaven. He is preparing us for the life and service yet to come. Nobody yet knows all that is in store for us in heaven, but this we do know; life today is a school in which God trains us for our future ministry in eternity." (W. Wiersbe, *Be Hopeful,* p. 34)

    b. According to 1 Peter 1:9, what is the future hope of our present-day faith?

4. Read 1 Peter 1:10-12. What were the prophets of the Old Testament inquiring about and searching for?

    a. As the prophets searched, who guided them so they knew what to prophesy? (vs. 11)

b. There are well over 300 Old Testament prophecies speaking to the events surrounding Jesus Christ, the coming Messiah. Many prophets spoke these words over a period of 500 years. The prophecies of His crucifixion were fulfilled within 24 hours. Look up the following verses and note what was prophesied concerning the Messiah.

Isaiah 35:5

Isaiah 53:5-7

Psalm 22:14,17

Daniel 9:24-26

c. Examine the cross below. In your own words, how is this visual a good representation of the concepts expressed in verses 10-12?

(FUTURE GLORY)

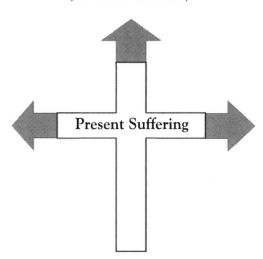

d. In verse 12 who has benefitted from the prophets' writings? Why would this be interesting to the angels who were observing the events?

A ACTING on God's Word

"For our citizenship is in heaven" Philippians 3:20a

There are many days I (Brenda) am painfully aware that as a believer in Jesus Christ, I will not fit into this world. My thoughts and actions are foreign to so many who I interact with daily. The things I witness make me shake my head in disbelief. What others easily embrace and accept, I simply cannot. Living here on earth is a constant reminder my citizenship is only temporary. I look forward to the day I will finally feel at home as a citizen of heaven.

1. I identified well with the audience Peter was writing to in chapter 1 because I, too, am a displaced pilgrim. How about you? When was the last time you felt like an alien living in a strange world? Describe the situation briefly below.

2. 1 Peter 1:3-5 are such encouraging verses regarding our hope in Christ and our future with Him. What stood out to you the most from these promises, and how will these truths help you the next time you feel like a foreigner?

3. Peter touched on the topic of suffering in 1 Peter 1:6-9. Alienation is one of the ways we might suffer as a pilgrim traveling through this world. Have you ever felt alienated? Describe. How might these verses comfort you during times of alienation?

4. Describe how we can lose track of the fact that this life and our present body should not be our primary focus.

   a. Based on what you learned today, what is the solution?

 **DELIGHTING** in God's Word

Looking back at our verses, how has the Lord prompted you to pray?

Write a verse from the chapter that God has spoken to your heart.

Close in Prayer

DELIGHTING
in the LORD
BIBLE STUDY SERIES

WEEK 2

LIVING A LIFE OF HOLINESS

1 Peter 1:13-25

It was early in the morning. Dim twilight exposed empty fishing nets at the bottom of Peter's boat. He and some of the disciples had just completed a night of unsuccessful fishing when suddenly Jesus appeared upon the shoreline. Peter immediately plunged into the sea when he recognized his Savior's arrival. Although Peter had previously seen the Lord resurrected, there remained unfinished business between them from the night Jesus was arrested. On that night, Peter denied knowing Jesus three times. He wept bitterly over his sin, but Jesus, knowing what was needed for Peter to experience full restoration, asked this simple and direct question, "Simon, son of Jonah, do you love me?" Jesus knew that if Peter was going to move forward and minister in His name, he needed to be not only cleansed from his past but also needed to be restored into fellowship once again.

Perhaps it was this very experience that echoed in Peter's mind as he wrote this chapter because he addresses both the need to be holy as well as to love both God and others. Peter reminds his readers it was Christ's precious blood which paid the penalty for our sinful indiscretions. Peter knew firsthand of Jesus' horrific death. He did not take the sacrifice of Jesus lightly and neither should we. It is our sins, along with the rest of humanity, which required this once and for all sacrifice. Jesus gave up everything! He left the perfection of heaven, lived among his broken and lost creation without sin, and then laid down His life so we could be forgiven. With this knowledge, how can we not pursue holiness? It is the least we can do out of our love and appreciation for all He has done for us.

Hebrews 12:14 says, "Pursue peace with all people, and holiness, without which no one will see the Lord." We must choose holiness if we want to be pleasing before our holy God. Holiness is a choice, and we must practice it even though we know we will fail at reaching for God's holy standard. Our text contains much to consider as Peter's abundance of knowledge spills out onto the page. As you open in prayer, ask God to cleanse you so that out of purity and love you may live and serve Him well.

RECEIVING God's Word

Open in Prayer

Read 1 Peter 1:13-25

EXPERIENCING God's Word

1. Read 1 Peter 1:13. Here we are given three commands for holy living. We have listed them for you below. Write these commands in your own words:

   a. Gird up the loins of your mind -

   b. Be sober (don't think just alcohol) -

   c. Rest your hope fully upon the grace that is to be brought to you at the revelation of Jesus Christ -

2. In verse 14 we are told not to conform ourselves to the former lusts as we ignorantly did before receiving Christ into our hearts as Lord and Savior. What does it mean to be conformed to something?

a. Read Romans 8:29. What conformity is desired?

3. Read 1 Peter 1:15-16. In the command given in these verses, Peter is quoting from Leviticus 20:7. *Holy* means "to be separated from sin and declared sacred to God as well as being set apart for a special and often higher end." God's very character is holiness. Given this definition, describe how our conduct should be affected.

4. Read 1 Peter 1:17-19. In verse 17 Peter uses the word *fear* as a guide for us as pilgrims in this world. Here the word *fear* means "a reverential fear of God which should cause a constant carefulness in our behavior." According to these verses, why should we fear God?

5. In 1 Peter 1:18-19 we are reminded of our salvation experience. Define redeemed. What were we redeemed from?

6. Read verses 18-21 and answer the following questions:

What were we not bought with? (v.18)

What were we bought with? (v.19)

Who put this plan into place and when? (v.20)

Why was this plan necessary? (v.21)

"We have been redeemed, not like Israel when they paid the half-shekel of silver - as in Exodus 30:12-15, as a ransom for their souls, or with gold - so often demanded as a ransom by some victorious leader when he dictated terms of peace to a conquered people, but we have been purchased and freed from judgment by the precious blood of Christ, and should no longer be conformed to the empty behavior of the past, which, while in accordance with ancestral customs, was opposed to the ways that glorify God." (H.A. Ironside, James and 1 and 2 Peter (Ironside Expository Commentaries), pg. 60

a. Why is it important for us to remember our salvation experience?

b. What did the Lord establish in order for us to remember what Christ did for us? Read 1 Corinthians 11:23-26 if you need help.

c. How is the conduct of the Jews described prior to their salvation in 1 Peter 1:18? What was the basis for their conduct?

7. According to verse 22, when our lives have been purified through Jesus Christ and we have been saved, love should be evident in our lives. The word *love* in this verse has two different meanings. The first meaning is "of brotherly love" and the second meaning is "of agape selfless love." Why might both types of love be necessary in the life of the believer? Why do they need to come from a pure heart?

a. Read Romans 12:9-21. Describe what love looks like through these verses.

b. Our ultimate example of love is seen in Jesus. Read Philippians 2:5-8. How did Jesus demonstrate love as described in these verses?

8. Read verse 23-25. Peter compares the corruptible things of this world to the incorruptible things of God. According to these verses, what things are corruptible? What things are incorruptible?

9. Last week we looked at how God the Father, Jesus the Son and the Holy Spirit are all active in our salvation. This week we see them active in our sanctification. Explain their roles from this week's verses.

ACTING on God's Word

When given the time and opportunity, I (Stacy) love antiquing. Not the kind of antiques that are perfectly carved and preserved with attractive adornments and pristine finishes garnering a high price tag. I like antiques that are aged and well worn, maybe with chipped paint and a rough edge; the ones that have character, uniqueness, and quality. Often the ones set apart from the rest. You know they've had purpose and are primed to be restored and used again, often in a whole new way.

Such is a picture of what God does with us. He sets us apart. He restores us. He determines our purpose, and all He asks is that we choose to take on His character by allowing Him to conform us to His image. Even in that, He does the refining work.

In our verses God's command came through loud and clear: "Be holy" in ALL your conduct which means your whole manner of living. Everything should be like Christ. He is holy and is our perfect example. His standard should be our aim. He isn't looking for the pristine outward finishes. He isn't looking for the perfectly polished with attractive adornments. He desires purity of heart deep within the heart of His daughters. So how do we do this? How does this translate to everyday life?

1. Peter talked about holiness in three places of our lives. I've listed them below. Try to be as specific as you can when answering. If you want, look up verses on your own for the second question regarding holiness in these areas of your lives.

<u>How do you struggle in this area? What does holiness look like in this area?</u>

Holy living in our minds

Holy living in our actions

Holy living in relationship with others

2. As we pursue holiness in our lives, obedience to God is required. Identify areas of your life where you are not being obedient to God. Are there any areas in your life where a past "unholy" lifestyle is still evident today? If so, identify those lifestyle choices. Before answering these questions, spend a minute sitting quietly before God and allow Him to speak into the places of your life and heart. As He speaks, list the thing(s) He is bringing to the surface. Then spend a minute confessing your sin before Him, allowing Him to cleanse and forgive.

Areas I'm not being obedient to God -

Unholy lifestyles -

Other -

3. Spend a few minutes in prayer and thank God for His gift of salvation. Remember all He has done for you. Make a list below of all the ways He has redeemed you.

a. He desires that you cultivate a life of holiness. This is to be our aim in all our conduct and manner of living. What tangible things can you do to cultivate a life of holiness?

D DELIGHTING in God's Word

Looking back at our verses, how has the Lord prompted you to pray?

Write a verse from the lesson God has spoken to your heart.

Close in Prayer

WEEK 3

LIVING STONES

1 Peter 2:1-12

It's the third year of Jesus' earthly ministry. Twelve ordinary men, many of different backgrounds and professions, have been selected as those 12 in Jesus' inner circle of students. They are eager to learn all they can from Jesus by observing His interactions and listening intently to His teachings. All the while they witnessed healings and amazing miracles performed in their midst. But there was so much to understand. Who was this God-man, Jesus? And why are the religious leaders plotting to destroy Him?

Jesus takes His 12 disciples and breaks away from the throngs of people in Galilee. He has something important to teach them, especially Peter. After much travel through dusty roads and grassy fields, Jesus stops. Before them stands a mountainous rock towering high to the clouds and massive in size. The place was Caesarea Philippi where pagan worship was both practiced and celebrated. The area is littered with idolatry.

While the world with its dead, idolatrous, religious systems stands as the backdrop, Jesus looks at Peter and asks him, "Who do you say that I am?" Peter, uncertain in his own mind but prompted by the Holy Spirit says, "You are the Christ, the Son of the Living God." And Jesus proceeds to tell Peter, his very name meaning stone, that he would be used by God to build the church on the rock of Jesus Christ. Peter, who was often brash, impulsive, outspoken, and overly enthusiastic, was chosen to do God's work as a living stone. God was working in Peter to grow Him spiritually and would use Peter to place stone upon stone in building God's spiritual house.

It is this very truth Peter is now teaching us. We are God's living stones, an oxymoron of words. Something so dead is now said to be alive. But isn't that what Christ does for us? We were dead in sin, yet by believing, we are now alive in Christ (Romans 6:11). To Him we are chosen, precious; a holy priesthood whom He desires to use as master builders to proclaim the truth of Jesus Christ.

I don't know about you, but sometimes I, Stacy, have trouble receiving the truth of who I am in Christ Jesus. Sometimes I just feel like a dead stone, forgetting that I am in fact filled with Christ's life and purpose. I am chosen by God, and God desires to build up in me a spiritual house of sacrifice and praise. Peter will tell us our job is to feed on His Word and to literally stay away from those things that pull us from Jesus. For all Jesus has done for us, it is our reasonable act of service to present our bodies to God as "living sacrifices, holy, and acceptable to God," Romans 12:1.

 **R** **RECEIVING** God's Word

Open in Prayer
Read 1 Peter 2:1-12

 **E** **EXPERIENCING** God's Word

1. Read 1 Peter 2:1. If we want to grow as a believer, we are told in this verse that we must lay aside some specific behaviors. What are they? Define them in your own words.

2. In verses 2-3 Peter makes the analogy between a believer and a newborn baby. From these verses, explain the relationship being made.

    a. How is the Word of God described?

b. Read 1 Corinthians 3:1-3. What hinders our ability to receive and digest God's Word? Connect the truths of 1 Corinthians 3 with those in 1 Peter 2:1.

> The failure to either desire or to receive this pure milk of the word is the reason for so many problems in both individual Christian lives and in congregations. "The sickly condition of so many Christians sets forth a lamentable complaint of the food with which they are supplied. To say nothing of strong meat, they do not even get milk. Hence the Church of God too much resembles the wards of a children's hospital." (David Guzik commentary, *Enduring Word*, quoting Meyer)

3. In 1 Peter 2:4 we see the words *living stone*. The word *living* is the Greek word *zao*. It means "not just human existence but fullness of life, both spiritual and eternal." It is a quality of life characteristic of vitality and power found in Jesus Christ. Keep this in mind as you consider the next analogy that Peter gives in verses 4-6. Describe this analogy. What does each word mean?

Who is THE Living Stone?_____

The house represents_____

Who are the other living stones?_____

How are they described? _____

What is their purpose?_____

Who is the chief cornerstone?_____

4. During Jesus' earthly ministry, He had many powerful interactions with Peter which we believe Peter draws from in this Epistle. One of these interactions is in Matthew 16:13-19 and sets the foundation for what Peter is teaching in the verses we are studying. Read Matthew 16:13-19 and answer the following questions:

a. What essential question did Jesus ask Peter?

b. What was Peter's answer?

c. How do you see the Holy Spirit working in this dialogue?

d. Look at verse 18. What is "this rock" upon which the church will be built?

e. Keep in mind that Peter's name means "stone." How will God use Peter as He builds His church?

5. Read Ephesians 2:19-22. How does this add to your understanding of what you have learned about living stones and the church?

6. Use 1 Peter 2:7-8 to compare how Jesus is received in these two verses by both groups of people.

   a. Why was "the word" the cause of stumbling?

7. How are we as believers described in 1Peter 2:9? Circle the description you appreciate most.

8. Read verse 10 and list the things that Christ has done for us.

9. In 1 Peter 2:11 Peter reminds us we are pilgrims and sojourners in this world. He also revisits the truth presented in 2:1-3. What does he say to us again?

   a. Why does he reinforce this point in verses 11-12?

   b. What is the ultimate goal for us as living stones? (vs.12)

A ACTING on God's Word

"But you are a chosen generation, a royal priesthood, a holy nation,
His own special people"
1 Peter 2:9

Brenda Ferri-Harris: Wife to Michael, mother of Rebecca and Ethan, daughter of Eugene and Carrie, and sister to Stephen.

These titles describe who I am within my immediate family. This is my place in my family's heritage. There is a measure of security and comfort knowing that I not only fit into this family line but also am known and loved by this group of people.

Brenda Ferri-Harris: chosen for my generation, a part of Christ's royal priesthood, a part of God's holy nation, and one of His special people.

The first description I gave of myself is likely the more common way I would depict myself. However, when I consider Peter's description of who I am in Christ, I recognize I belong to yet another family line that supersedes my earthly ancestry. I have never introduced myself to anyone with those titles associated with my name. How about you? Have you ever stopped to really consider your relationship and title within God's family?

The four titles Peter gives his readers in 1 Peter 2:9 are powerful and worth investigating. Let's look at how these titles were given to a select group of people in the Old Testament, and then we'll look at how these concepts have been applied in New Testament times to those who have put their faith in Jesus Christ. As we do this, I pray it will affect how you see yourself and define who you are in God's family.

1. *Chosen Generation*

Deuteronomy 10:15
The Lord delighted only in your fathers, to love them; and He chose their descendants after them, you above all peoples, as it is this day.

Ephesians 1:4-5
Just as He chose us in Him before the foundation of the world, that we should be holy and without blame before Him in love, having predestined us to adoption as sons by Jesus Christ to Himself, according to the good pleasure of His will.

a. Based on these verses, how are you part of a chosen generation?

b. How does this impact your view of yourself?

2. *Royal Priesthood*

Exodus 40:15
You shall anoint them, as you anointed their father, that they may minister to Me as priests; for their anointing shall surely be an everlasting priesthood throughout their generations.

Revelation 1:5-6
And from Jesus Christ, the faithful witness, the firstborn from the dead, and the ruler over the kings of the earth. To Him who loved us and washed us from our sins in His own blood, and has made us kings and priests to His God and Father, to Him be glory and dominion forever and ever. Amen.

a. The job of the priest was to go before the Lord on behalf of the people for worship and sacrifice. Why is a priest no longer needed today for this role?

b. How are you a part of God's royal priesthood today?

c. How does this impact your relationship with God?

3. <u>*Holy Nation*</u>

   Exodus 19:6
   And you shall be to Me a kingdom of priests and a holy nation. These are the words which you shall speak to the children of Israel.

   Ephesians 2:10
   For we are His workmanship, created in Christ Jesus for good works, which God prepared beforehand that we should walk in them.

   a. How do you see yourself as part of God's holy nation?

b.   How does this impact your life?

4. <u>*His Own Special People*</u>

Deuteronomy 7:6
For you are a holy people to the Lord your God; the Lord your God has chosen you to be a people for Himself, a special treasure above all the peoples on the face of the earth.

Ephesians 1:4-6
Just as He chose us in Him before the foundation of the world, that we should be holy and without blame before Him in love, having predestined us to adoption as sons by Jesus Christ to Himself, according to the good pleasure of His will, to the praise of the glory of His grace, by which He made us accepted in the Beloved.

a.   How does this impact how you see yourself?

b.   How does this impact your interactions with God's other "special people?"

 **DELIGHTING** in God's Word

Looking back at our verses, how has the Lord prompted you to pray?

Write a verse from the lesson God has spoken to your heart.

Close in Prayer

DELIGHTING
in the LORD
BIBLE STUDY SERIES

WEEK 4

YOU WANT ME TO DO WHAT?

1 Peter 2:13-25

The crowd was pressing in to listen to Jesus teach the Word of God. Perhaps to gain a little personal space as well as to magnify His voice to the growing crowd, Jesus scanned the shoreline and saw two empty fishing boats. Peter was washing his nets on the shore when Jesus stepped into his boat and asked him to push out a little way into Lake Gennesaret. Because Peter complied, he ended up with a front row seat to the teaching. When the formal lesson for the crowd ended, a very personal lesson began for Peter. The lesson began like this, "Launch out into the deep and let down your nets for a catch."

What ran through Peter's mind when he heard this command? Did he think to himself, "You want me to do what? I just fished all night and caught nothing. Clearly, you don't know much about the trade of fishing because it is daytime, and we don't catch fish during the day."

Peter's thoughts were not recorded in the Bible, but his submissive response was written onto the pages of Luke 5 with him saying, "Master, we have toiled all night and caught nothing; nevertheless, at Your word I will let down the net." You probably know what happened next. Peter caught so many fish, the net nearly broke. Peter's small, submissive act forever changed the trajectory of his life. That day Peter would put his hope in Christ and leave everything behind to follow Him. There would be many more lessons ahead for Peter regarding the act of submission, but this was the first. It was simple, relatively easy to do, and Peter had nothing to lose by following Jesus' directions. However, later in his life, the acts of submission would become increasingly more difficult and eventually cost him his life. We will be spending time this week and next week studying the topic of submission. This is not a popular subject, and for some, it can be downright uncomfortable to study, let alone obey. No matter how you feel about submission, in the end the key to remember is that obedience boils down to only two people, God and you. Behind every leader asking for compliance, stands God alone. We would do well to remember our obedience pleases Him.

RECEIVING God's Word

Open in Prayer

Read 1 Peter 2:13-25

EXPERIENCING God's Word

Experience 1: 1 Peter 2:13-17

1. In 1 Peter 2:13-14 what command is given, and why are we told to follow it?

2. Look up the following verses about submission and note what you learn:

   James 4:7

   Ephesians 5:21

   1 Corinthians 11:3

   Romans 13:1-7

"Submit is the overriding action required of believers. The word means 'to place yourself under someone, to rank under someone.' Here it is essentially a synonym for obedience. Of course, submission to authority does not involve actions that are sinful or contrary to the Word of God. The believer is to obey except when commanded to sin. This is the Christian's responsibility toward all forms of human authority." (Holman)

3. Read 1 Peter 2:15-17 and answer the following questions:

   a. What incentives are given to be submissive?

   b. How can submission protect us?

   c. The enemy wants us to believe submission is bondage, but according to verse 16, what are we?

   d. Peter describes believers as bondservants of God. Describe what you think bondservant means in your own words and how this title affects your ability to submit to a leader.

e. In verse 17 we are given four direct commands. List them in order of Biblical submission below:

1)

2)

3)

4)

Experience 2: 1 Peter 2:18-25

1. Read 1 Peter 2:18-19. Under what conditions does a servant need to submit to their master and why?

> The practice of slavery was a well-entrenched part of the culture of the first century, and the Bible contains no direct command or call to abolish slavery. The implications of the gospel, especially the ethic of love, stand clearly in opposition to slavery." (Holman)

> "*Oiketai*, servants, means member of a household, domestic servants, including free-men as well as slaves. What Peter has primarily in mind are not slaves as a class, but the household as a common social institution." Alan M. Stibbs, *The First Epistle General of Peter,* p. 114.

2. Read 1 Peter 2:20 and Matthew 5:43-47. Compare these two verses and the main concept being explained.

3. According to 1 Peter 2:20, what type of behavior is commendable before God when submitting to someone in authority?

4. Christ is the perfect example of how to endure suffering from unfair and harsh authority figures. Read verses 22-23 and list how Christ responded when He was unjustly and severely treated by earthly masters.

   a. God is ultimately the judge of all evil. Read Romans 12:19. How can we take comfort from the truth found in this verse when we bear up under a difficult authority in our lives?

5. In verse 24 we are reminded of Jesus' death for our sins. Fill in the blanks from verse 24. We having died to _____, might live for

_____.

a. Explain how Jesus' stripes have brought us healing.

6. Peter gives us the picture of sheep under the authority of the Shepherd. How is the Shepherd described in verse 25?

a. Read Psalm 23. List below how Jesus, as our Shepherd, comforts His sheep in times of great difficulty.

7. In verses 24 & 25 Peter is quoting from Isaiah 53:4-6. Here we see Jesus as a suffering servant. Why do you think Peter quoted from Isaiah? What point was he trying to make to his readers?

A ACTING on God's Word

A few years ago, a craft store chain learned the insurance they were offering their employees allowed for contraception that induced abortions. The craft store's owners are professing believers in Jesus Christ. Upon learning of this insurance provision, they quickly had the insurance company drop this coverage from their employee's plans. Doing this was in direct violation of the governmental policy in place under the Affordable Care Act. For the owner, David Green, that didn't matter. He could not offer his employees the means to end the life of another human being. That would be in direct violation to God's commands, and before David would submit to the government, he had to submit to God, knowing what God's Word required.

A lawsuit ensued. I'm sure a great deal of money was spent in their defense. They were personally and professionally under attack in the mainstream media, but ultimately, the Green family won in a landmark court case in their favor. God's law was upheld over earthly law.

This week we looked closely at submission and the difficulty in submitting to an unjust master. Submission is often a difficult and unpopular topic for people. It is especially difficult to tell some to submit to someone who exerts authority with a hard heart and heavy hand. What we saw in these verses were the answer to the why's and how's of submission.

1. From what you learned, why is submission required by God, and how are we able to submit to those who may be unjustly or unfairly treating us?

2. God requires His servants to submit to the government authorities placed over us. This includes local and national politicians, law enforcement officials, and judges. Has it ever been challenging for you to submit to the government authorities over you? Explain.

3. Peter taught us the servant/master model prevalent in the culture at that time. Since the Greek word for servant is more general in its meaning, it can apply to any worker/supervisor situation. Have you ever worked for someone who treated you unjustly or harshly? Explain.

   a. Were you able to submit to their authority in a Christ-like manner? If not, what have you learned that you could apply to this type of situation in the future?

4. Our attitude matters in submission. Sometimes we can act like we are submitting, but really our heart is in rebellion. Under each heading, list the attitudes that could accompany the act of submitting or not submitting:

Submitting to an unjust Master	Not submitting to an unjust master
List possible attitudes	List possible attitudes
example:	**example:**
Humble	Defensive

5. What, if anything, is your greatest challenge in submission? What have you learned that can help with these challenges?

D   DELIGHTING in God's Word

Looking back at our verses, how has the Lord prompted you to pray?

Write a verse from the lesson God has spoken to your heart.

Close in Prayer

WEEK 5

WITHOUT A WORD

1 Peter 3:1-7

Nine disciples stayed behind as Jesus took Peter, James and John up a mountain to pray with Him. The disciples thought they were going up the mountain to simply pray, but Jesus knew there would be more to this meeting. This prayer time with the Lord would be like none other. The group had been praying, but Luke 9:32 describes Peter and the other disciples as being "heavy with sleep." That feeling quickly dissipated when they realized this was not a typical prayer meeting.

There in front of them stood Jesus with an altered appearance. His face shone like the sun, and his clothes were white and glistening. Jesus had two guests standing with Him, Moses and Elijah. The disciples were bewildered as they tried to grasp what they were seeing. When Moses and Elijah turn to leave, Peter speaks up impetuously. Seeing those gathered, Peter thinks it's a good idea for everyone to hang out a little while longer! He tells Jesus, "Master, it's good for us to be here, let us make three tabernacles; one for You, one for Moses and one for Elijah." Every Biblical account of this event explains Peter did not know what he was suggesting to Jesus, and then all of a sudden a voice from heaven said, "This is My beloved Son. Hear Him." It was as if God was telling Peter to be quiet and listen rather than speak. As soon as the voice stopped, everything returned to normal. Jesus was alone and no longer glowing. Luke 9:36 records their response to the events they witnessed under the instruction of Jesus, "But they kept quiet and told no one in those days any of the things they had seen."

Ecclesiastes 3:7 says, "There is a time to keep silent and a time to speak," and oh, how I (Brenda) think most of us can relate to the unfortunate times when we have mismanaged these communication tools. If only God had given us a holy hush like He did Peter on the mountain of transfiguration! Words hold power, and if anyone knows that, it is Peter. In our text he shares solid wisdom for wives and husbands about submission, speech, conduct, and prayer. In a marriage relationship, it is a beautiful thing to see a wife and a husband honor each other with their words and actions. May we be humble enough to see where we fall short, be willing to change where necessary, and know that our obedience demonstrates our love for the Lord and our spouse.

RECEIVING God's Word

Open in Prayer

Read 1 Peter 3:1-7

EXPERIENCING God's Word

1. In 1 Peter 3:1 believing wives are the focus and submission is the command.

   a. Fill in the blank for 3:1a. "_____, likewise, be _____ to your _____ husbands." (NKJV)

   b. How is the command in verse 1a exclusive?

   c. Read Ephesians 5:22-24. Why is the command in verse 1a important as a function of order within the home? What is the order given in these verses?

   d. Describe the spiritual condition of this husband in verse 1. What words in this verse brought you to this conclusion?

e. How will silence impact this husband spiritually?

2. Read 1 Peter 3:1b-2. The word *conduct* used in verse 1 and 2 means "lifestyle." As a believing wife, our lifestyle should be chaste with a reverential fear of God. According to the definition of chaste, a chaste lifestyle is one that is uncontaminated. Describe a contaminated lifestyle. How could this be detrimental to a marriage?

a. Why is reverential fear linked with chaste conduct?

> "The powerful purity of a godly woman's life can soften even the stoniest male heart without a word (Titus 2:5)." *(Bible Knowledge Commentary p.848)*

3. Read 1 Peter 3:3-4. Outward and inward commands are being given. Fill in the chart from what you see in these two verses. (Note: Some boxes will remain empty.)

Verse	Outward	Inward (Incorruptible beauty)
Verse 3		
Verse 4		

a. Is verse 3 suggesting that outward adornments are wrong? Explain.

b. In the context of a marriage relationship, how can the "hidden person of the heart" who has a gentle and quiet spirit impact the non-believing husband toward the Lord?

> "The word gentle has a caress in it; yet behind gentleness stands the strength of steel. The supreme characteristic of the "gentle" woman is that she lives under perfect control. She is not given to panic, but exudes great strength. "Quiet," too, suggests being under control. It also means "to evidence a calming influence." Together, the two words speak of strength of character, strong, self-control, describing a person of quiet elegance and dignity." (Holman New Testament Commentary 1 & 2 Peter, pg. 49)

4. Read 1 Peter 3:5. Peter looks into history for examples of godly wives. What is the main characteristic seen in a holy woman according to verse 5?

   a. Why is this characteristic needed in order to obey God's command to submit to our husbands?

5. Read 1 Peter 3:6. Submission is a choice. It is an act of obedience to God. Peter uses Sarah as an example for us to follow. According to this verse, how do we know Sarah submitted to her husband? Keep in mind that this title would have been in line with the culture of that time. How would this title represent a submissive heart?

6. Let's look at Sarai's example further. Read Genesis 12:10-20 and answer the following questions:

   a. There is a famine in Canaan, and Abram leaves with Sarai, his wife, for Egypt. In verses 12-13 what does Abram tell his wife to do and why?

   b. According to verses 14-16, Sarai obeyed despite the detrimental consequences that came to her. Read verses 17-20. How did God protect Sarai?

7. In 1 Peter 3:6 fear stands in direct contrast to faith. Faith in God, like Sarah's, sets us within her spiritual heritage. How does fear hinder us from submitting to God and our husbands?

8. In 1 Peter 3:7 Peter now looks at the godly husband. What three commands are given for the husband to follow?

9. In verse 7 Peter points out that believing husbands and wives need to remember that their relationship is not just one of a physical union but also something spiritual that comes with great blessing. What word does Peter use to describe their spiritual inheritance, and what is the joint blessing?

   a. How should this spiritual relationship and inheritance affect the marriage and the individual commands God gives to husbands and wives?

10. In verse 7 Peter points out to godly husbands the possible consequence of not living as a godly husband. What is this possible consequence?

"The weakness in view here is primarily physical weakness, since the term vessel means the human body." (NKJV Study Bible, p 1986)

ACTING on God's Word

It was another perfect day in the Garden of Eden as God witnessed the beauty of His creation and design. The first marriage ceremony was performed. It was probably the simplest ceremony, yet the most beautiful in all of history. Sin had not entered the scene to mar the landscape and corrupt the hearts of husband and wife. Genesis 18 tells us God knew Adam needed a helper. It was not good for him to be alone. In His infinite knowledge and wisdom, God created Eve from the rib of Adam. Eve was not to be a footstool for Adam as she wasn't created from the foot bone. Eve was not to be a handmaiden either, nor was she to be the head over him. No, the bone used to create Eve was Adam's rib bone; the bone that encased Adam's heart.

Upon completion, God brought Eve to Adam. She was hand-picked and handmade just for Adam. If you're married, you and your husband are no different. Adam and Eve became one flesh that day living in God's perfection and enjoying His blessings. That all quickly changed when Eve decided to disobey God. You know the story; she chose to eat from the one tree God commanded her to leave alone. Adam chose to eat as well, and from that one choice of the will, the one choice that opposed God, sin entered into creation as well as marriage. Sin has consequences. God set forth consequences for men as well as women. Genesis 3:16 tells us that one of these consequences would be a woman's desire to rule over her husband.

Even today that consequence still plagues us as women and wives. The desire for power and authority affects many marriages. Maybe you've heard it said, "She wears the pants in that family," meaning the wife is in charge. In our verses we studied God's command to believing wives in relationship to their husbands, specifically unbelieving husbands, regarding submission. The questions below are addressed to wives. If you are not currently a wife, skip to the last application question.

1. God's command to wives regarding submission is the same whether the husband is saved or unsaved. Why is submission often a difficult topic to accept and obey? Why could it be especially challenging when you are a believer but your husband is not?

    a. On the scale below rate yourself in the area of submission to your husband.

1_____5_____10
Never submit   Always submit

    b. Why did you give yourself that rating? If your rating was not 10, what keeps you from submitting to your husband as God commands?

2. When Eve sinned and God gave consequences, authority and control were two areas women would forever struggle against. So often we try to control our husbands and/or exert authority over them. Name some different ways women do this.

3. In our verses Peter admonished wives concerning their unbelieving husbands and their influence over them. This can also apply to all wives. What is our most powerful influence on our husbands? From what you learned, explain how this is a powerful witness of God's love.

4. There is beauty and blessing in God's design. We get to experience this when we obey God's commands fully. So often we want to change our husbands to experience God's blessing when God wants to change each of us. We are responsible for our obedience to God. Ask God to show you how you can more fully obey his command regarding submission. If there is an area God is showing you, the first step is often asking for forgiveness. Once you've done this with God, I encourage you to do the same with your husband.

5. What area addressed in this week's lesson do you find yourself struggling with the most? Check all that apply.

    _____Holding my tongue

    _____Pure lifestyle

    _____Focusing too much on the physical and not the spiritual

    _____Having a gentle and quiet spirit

    _____Trusting God with my marriage and/or husband's salvation

    What did you learn this week that can help you overcome through Christ in this area?

6. There are times in life when we have blind spots or veiled vision. Go to your husband and ask him how you are doing in the area of submission. Ask him for his perspective on ways you could submit and respect him better.

7. If you are single, divorced or widowed, how would you take the lesson, and use it to disciple and instruct a young wife in godly marriage principles?

****If you are in an abusive relationship, this is outside God's design. God commands husbands to love their wives as Christ loved the church and gave His life for her (Ephesians 5:25). Love does not involve abuse. If you are in an abusive relationship, please let your DITL leader know or contact the local abuse hotline.

 **DELIGHTING** in God's Word

Looking back at our verses, how has the Lord prompted you to pray?

Write a verse from the lesson that God has spoken to your heart.

Close in Prayer

DELIGHTING
in the LORD
BIBLE STUDY SERIES

WEEK 6

SO SIMPLE, BUT SO HARD

1 Peter 3:8-12

It was a significant night, a night that began in an upper room overlooking Jerusalem. The 12 disciples gathered with Jesus to share the Passover meal. But it was different this time. As they ate and drank, Jesus exposed the evil in the heart of one of the disciples. A murmuring ran through those seated followed by disbelief, questions, and sorrow. Called out by Jesus for the wickedness in his heart and unable to stay with them any longer, Judas leaves.

As the meal progressed, Jesus took the bread and the wine and told them a new covenant between God and His people was being established. I (Stacy) would imagine it was confusing and comforting all at the same time for the disciples. What did this mean? And why would Jesus "never" have this meal with them again in Jerusalem?

The meal comes to an end, and Jesus motions for the 11 to come with Him to the Mount of Olives. They cross the Kidron Valley and make their way to Gethsemane. Darkness is permeating the air; the moon glistening to light their way. Jesus motions again to His beloved. "Sit here while I pray," Mark 14:32. He looks at Peter, James, and John and tells them they are to follow Him further into the garden. Jesus' heart is in anguish. The disciples sense something and stay close to Jesus. They keep walking as Jesus turns to them and says, "My soul is exceedingly sorrowful, even to death. Stay here and watch," (Mark 14:34). The disciples obey as Jesus moves alone further into the heart of Gethsemane.

Jesus' hour of death was quickly approaching. The cross loomed in the immediate future. Yet the disciples, oblivious to the suffering awaiting Jesus, were overcome with sleep. Their eyes grew heavy while their Savior was sweating drops of blood from crying out in distress to God, His Father. Jesus gave them two simple commands: stay here and keep watch. So simple, yet so hard. Tiredness, full stomachs, and selfishness took over as their eyes closed, and they drifted off to sleep.

It wasn't but an hour when Jesus abruptly awoke them. Coming to Peter, Jesus says, "Simon, are you sleeping? Could you not watch one hour? Watch and pray; lest you enter into temptation. The spirit is indeed willing but the flesh is weak" (Mark 14:38). Peter tries as hard as he can, but two more times the flesh wins and sleep results. It was too late. Jesus' accusers were coming as the sound of rattling swords echoed in the distance.

What Jesus asked of Peter, James, and John wasn't hard. Why couldn't they do it? They loved Jesus. They watched Jesus serve others tirelessly, compassionately, and tenderly for three years. Yet when Jesus needed them, they failed to serve Him the way He had served them for so long.

This week we are only going to cover five verses. These are power-packed verses calling for obedience. Peter, knowing that with obedience comes inherited blessing (Acts 5:32), exhorts us to live like Jesus. At face value these commands are simple. In action, they are a whole lot harder. It is only through the power of the Holy Spirit and choosing to obey that we can live this way. It is a challenge for all of us, including me, Stacy. But remember, as weak as the flesh is, the Spirit is always willing to help.

RECEIVING God's Word

Open in Prayer
Read 1 Peter 3:8-12

EXPERIENCING God's Word

1. Peter starts verse 8 with the word *finally*, and he is wrapping up his exhortation about submission. In 1 Peter 3:8 who is Peter speaking to? (Recall everyone Peter has been addressing in the previous chapter as well as this one.)

a. There is so much in 1 Peter 3:8 that in order not to miss anything we are going to break the verse into sections. These sections come as a series of commands. The commands are:

- Be of one mind (3:8a)
- Have compassion for one another (3:8b)
- Love as brothers (3:8c)
- Be tenderhearted (3:8d)
- Be courteous (3:8e)

"Be of one mind" (3:8a)

2. 1 Peter 3:8a suggests we must be of one mind first. Read 1 Corinthians 2:9-16 and answer the following questions:

a. God wants to give us His wisdom. What are the things He wants us to know according to verse 9?

b. Who imparts this knowledge to us and how? (v.10-12)

c. Compare the mind of the natural man with the mind of the spiritual man (v. 13-15)

d. In verse 16 a powerful statement is made about the believer's mind. Write 1 Corinthians 2:16b below. Think about the fact that this is a promise given to all those who have put their trust in Christ!

1 Corinthians 2:16b:

"But we _____ "

e. From what you learned, what does it mean to be of one mind?

"Have compassion for one another" (3:8b)

3. Read the following verses about compassion and note what you learn.

a. Galatians 6:2

b. Colossians 3:12

c. 1 Thessalonians 5:11-14

d. Luke 7:13-17. Describe how Jesus demonstrated His heart of compassion in this account.

e. From what you learned, what does compassion look like in the life of a believer?

"Love as brothers" (3:8c)

4. Read Romans 12:10-13. We are told in this verse to love each other. List the specific actions suggested in this verse.

a. Read John 15:12-17. Describe how Jesus fulfilled the very command He gave in these verses.

b. In your own words, what does brotherly love look like?

"Be tenderhearted" (3:8d)

5. Read Ephesians 4:32. How are we encouraged to live according to this verse?

6. Jesus is always our example to follow. Read the following verses and note who received Jesus' tenderheartedness.

    a. Matthew 9:36

    b. Matthew 14:14

    c. Mark 8:2

    d. Mark 9:22-25

    e. John 11:33

7. Explain simply what it means to be tenderhearted.

Be courteous (3:8e)

8. Read Ruth 2:8-16. Ruth was widowed. She left Moab with her mother-in-law, Naomi, who was also widowed. They had no financial means. From what you read, how did Boaz, who was a type of Christ, demonstrate courteousness toward Ruth?

9. How would you explain to someone else what it means to be courteous based on these verses?

10. Read 1 Peter 3:9. In this verse we read about perhaps one of the most difficult things to do as a Christian. What is it? How are we commanded to respond?

a. Read Matthew 5:43-48. Jesus summarizes here what Peter has presented to us in 1 Peter 3:9. What is the standard Jesus is setting forth for those who hurt/wrong us? If we follow what Jesus has commanded here, what are we told will result?

"The natural response to hostility is retaliation. This is what the terrible ethnic conflicts all over the world are all about – one group wrongs another, and dedicates the rest of its existence to repaying that wrong. Only the love of Jesus for our enemies can break the terrible cycle." (David Guzik)

11. 1 Peter 3:9 tells us this manner of living is necessary for the believer because the believer was called to it once they accepted Christ into their heart. God promises us a blessing for obedience. Notice the word used in verse 9. We inherit the blessing. Explain why it is inherited and not earned?

12. 1 Peter 3:10-12 is quoting Psalm 34:12-16. This text could be a summation of the rules for living a long and happy life. List the five "rules" in these verses.

    a. What two things do we learn about God from these verses? How does this bring encouragement to you as you seek to live for the Lord?

 **ACTING** on God's Word

Have you ever heard this phrase, "It's so simple, just read the directions, you'll get it" only to find when you went to complete the "simple task," you couldn't complete step number one? I (Brenda) have this experience not only with physical tasks but also at times when I try to follow spiritual commands Jesus gave us in the Bible. For example, in Mark 12:31 Jesus says, "Love your neighbor as yourself." Simple and straightforward, right? But how does that work out when the neighbor's dog barks incessantly at 11pm, and you are trying to fall asleep? Or how about when your neighbor decides to put up a political sign that disagrees with your view of politics? Or when your neighbor buys a gargantuan boat and parks it in their driveway alongside the RV they own which houses their relatives during the week of Thanksgiving? What then? How loving are you feeling? The command is so simple, yet so hard. But why?

1. Read the list of "simple" commands we were given in 1 Peter 3:8-12. Put a check mark next to the ones you feel you are able to do most of the time and circle the ones you feel are a struggle for you.

   - Be compassionate
   - Be loving
   - Be tenderhearted
   - Be courteous
   - Do not return evil for evil
   - Do not speak deceit
   - Turn from evil; do good
   - Seek peace and purse it

2. If you circled any of the commands on the previous page, what justification might you make for your behavior(s)? Write the justifications below.

3. Perhaps another basic reason we may disobey God's simple commands is because we do not have the heartfelt conviction that obeying God will bring the blessing He promises. Reread 1 Peter 3:9-11. Do you doubt the blessings of God that come from obedience? If so, explain to the Lord why you doubt Him. Ask Him to help you with your unbelief.

4. In John 14:26 Jesus promised us help when He said, "But the Helper, the Holy Spirit, whom the Father will send in My name, He will teach you all things and bring to your remembrance all the things that I said to you." God has provided us with the Holy Spirit. How has His help allowed you to experience victory over the simple yet hard-to-do things in the past? Now take that triumph and apply it to something you are struggling with today. Ask God for His help and strength to overcome in His name.

D DELIGHTING in God's Word

Looking back at our verses, how has the Lord prompted you to pray?

Write a verse from the lesson God has spoken to your heart.

Close in Prayer

WEEK 7

BE READY

1 Peter 3:13-22

A little over forty days had passed since Peter witnessed Jesus' gruesome and painful death. The cross that held Jesus stood empty as Jesus' limp and lifeless body was laid to rest in a secure tomb. Three days later that tomb was empty. Peter saw it firsthand. All that remained in the tomb were Jesus' linen burial cloths. More proof of Jesus' resurrection would come as Peter would see his risen Lord again and again in the days after His resurrection.

One final meeting with Jesus awaited Peter in Jerusalem. Peter and the other disciples gathered and waited with eagerness for Jesus' instructions. Was Jesus now going to restore the kingdom to Israel? Was their Messiah going to rule as King? The meeting didn't go the way they thought it would. As they sat around the table, Jesus opened the Scriptures to them and gave them understanding in Spiritual truths. And then came the command: Be ready (Acts 1:8). The command was to the point; be ready to receive the power of the Holy Spirit and be ready to be witnesses to the power of the resurrected Christ in Jerusalem and beyond.

The meeting was done. The infallible proofs of Jesus' resurrection completed. Jesus got up from the table and beckoned for them to follow Him. Leading them outside Jerusalem, they walked the next two miles to the southeastern slope of the Mount of Olives. Jesus stopped once they reached the town of Bethany. Turning to His disciples, Jesus lifted His hands toward Heaven and prayed a blessing over those men who were entrusted with the message of the Gospel. A message of hope, forgiveness, love, and grace; offering an abundant and eternal life. When Jesus finished speaking, Peter saw Jesus taken up into a cloud (Acts 1:9). Peter's eyes stared intently up into the sky as two men quickly interrupted the moment. Their words were ones of comfort. "This same Jesus, Who was taken up from you into heaven, will so come in like manner as you saw Him go into heaven" (Acts 1:11). There was work for the disciples to do as they waited.

I, Stacy, imagine as Peter wrote of the things we will study that his mind recalled his early days of ministry; the defenses made of the gospel, the miracles, and the power of the gospel of Christ. But those memories were also entangled with the suffering and persecution that came from the message being both lived and preached. Living out his last days, Peter tells us it's all worth it by saying, "even if you suffer for righteousness sake, you are blessed" (1 Peter 3:14). With urgency and conviction, Peter tells us to "be ready to tell people about this hope within you." A hope grounded on the historical reality of the resurrected Christ. Jesus led the way, and because of Him, there is no uncertainty affecting our hope in Him or our future. It's a message people need to hear. Will you let your life be Christ's witness? Will you openly speak of your hope in Christ even if it means suffering or persecution? Are you ready?

RECEIVING God's Word

Open in Prayer
Read 1 Peter 3:13-22

EXPERIENCING God's Word

Experience 1: 1 Peter 3:13-17

1. In 1 Peter 3:13 Peter is presenting us with a question. Put that question in your own words. What is the essence of his question?

2. Peter takes suffering and blessing and puts them together in verse 14. This is a common theme in Scripture. Peter also quotes Isaiah 8:12 to support this spiritual truth. Read Isaiah 8:11-14. God is speaking to the prophet Isaiah. What point is God making about fear, suffering, and blessing?

3. The word *sanctify* in 1 Peter 3:15 speaks of "being set apart as holy; to dedicate, purify and consecrate unto God." What does it mean to sanctify the Lord God in your heart?

   a. When we sanctify God in our hearts, how does this help us in times of suffering?

4. Before a witness takes the stand in a court trial, a lawyer prepares the witness by going over questions and answers. Similarly, Peter is telling believers in verse 15 to always be ready to give a defense for their faith. Why is this important, and how can you be prepared?

Week 7: Be Ready

a. Meekness and fear are important when sharing our faith with others. How do gentleness (meekness) and respect (fear) speak powerfully as you witness to others?

5. Read 1 Peter 3:16. How does a good conscience bring comfort and peace when people speak poorly about you, defame you, or attack your character? Go back to 1 Peter 2:23. How did Christ demonstrate this for us?

6. Read 1 Peter 3:17. Suffering can come to the believer either through doing good or evil. Explain.

a. Read Galatians 6:9. How is this an encouragement?

b. Read Matthew 5:10-12. What spiritual truth is given in this verse?

Experience 2: 1 Peter 3:18-22

1. How is the gospel summed up in 1 Peter 3:18?

2. Read 1 Peter 3:19-20. These can be difficult verses to understand. Bible scholars vary on their interpretation of these verses. We will be taking the interpretation widely held by Calvary Chapel pastors. In order to gain deeper understanding with the phrase "by whom also He went and preached to the spirits in prison," we need to look at the specific words and their meaning. *Preached* is "kerysso" in the Greek. It means "to make a proclamation or to officiate as a herald." Regarding the *spirits in prison*, the word *spirits* refers to angels in the spiritual realm in this verse. These are angels that have fallen from heaven. They were disobedient according to v.20.

   a. Who are these spirits? Read Genesis 6:1-4. Something horrible and hard to truly understand happened in the days of Noah. Angels in the angelic realm tried to cohabit with humanity. This caused corruption. What resulted based on these verses?

   b. Read Jude 6. What do you further learn about these fallen angels?

c. Following Christ's death, He made a proclamation to these angels. We don't know what this proclamation was specifically, but we can have a good idea based on the context of 1 Peter 3:18-22. Read 1 Peter 3:22. What does this verse suggest about the message of Jesus' proclamation?

d. In verse 20 the "Divine longsuffering" is God. Go back to Genesis 6:5-12 & 7:1. Why would God be described this way based on what is happening with mankind? What is God's solution?

3. In 1 Peter 3:21 Peter speaks of baptism in connection with Noah and his family being saved from the flood through the ark. Noah had a clear conscience before God and so should we. Read Romans 6:3-6. What does baptism represent? Does baptism save us? Explain.

a. How is baptism the evidence of a clear conscience before God?

b. How would the story of Noah be an encouragement to the small group of persecuted Christians suffering at the time Peter was writing this letter?

> The flood pictures death, burial, and resurrection. The waters buried the earth in judgment, but they also lifted Noah and his family up to safety. The early church saw in the ark a picture of salvation. Noah and his family were saved by faith because they believed God and entered into the ark of safety, so sinners are saved by faith when they trust Christ and become one with Him. (Warren Wiersbe, *Be Hopeful*, pg. 108)

4. According to 1 Peter 3:22, where is Jesus now? Who does He have authority over?

A ACTING on God's Word

"...and <u>always</u> be ready to give a defense to everyone who asks you a reason for the hope that is within you..." 1 Peter 3:15

When Stacy and I go away to write a Bible study, we have to get ready. We check our calendars for open dates, set up accommodations to stay for several nights, make meals in advance, buy commentaries on the subject we are studying, and of course, pack our suitcases with clothes. Then on the day we leave for our trip, we feel prepared to go away and work. The trips don't miraculously come together. We must put in time and effort to get ready to be away. I (Brenda) see a parallel between being prepared to travel and being prepared to share my faith. Peter encourages us to be ready to give a defense to anyone who asks about our hope in Jesus Christ but that takes preparation and planning.

<u>**Be Prepared to Answer**</u>

1. We cannot possibly be ready for every question that may be asked of us, but it is important to have some solid answers to defend your faith and explain your hope. How would you answer these questions? Wherever possible, back up your answers with Scripture.

    a.   You really believe the Bible is true? How can it be if humans wrote it down?

    b.   God is loving so He won't send good people to hell, right?

    c.   You believe in a literal devil? Is he in hell right now?

    d.   What is the point to life? Why am I even here?

e. How do you know God exists at all since you cannot see Him, feel Him, or touch Him?

2. Is there a question you have been asked, and at the time you did not feel ready to answer it? What was it?

   a. Investigate ways to answer that question now through your Bible or plan to discuss this question with your small group.

3. When was the last time you looked for opportunities to share the gospel? What were the circumstances, and how did the opportunity unfold?

Be Prepared to Suffer

4. The answers you give to the previous questions could cause divisions, suffering, and perhaps persecution. Have you ever avoided sharing your faith because you didn't feel like dealing with adverse reactions? Why or why not?

   a. What did Peter tell us in our text about being ready for suffering and persecution? Have you ever experienced either one, if so when?

5. How can being prepared with answers to these and other questions potentially mean the difference between life and death spiritually? How does this encourage you to spend the time to be ready in the future to answer unbelievers who God allows to intersect with your life?

 DELIGHTING in God's Word

Looking back at our verses, how has the Lord prompted you to pray?

Write a verse from the lesson God has spoken to your heart.

Close in Prayer

DELIGHTING
in the LORD
BIBLE STUDY SERIES

WEEK 8

THE CLOCK IS TICKING

1 Peter 4:1-11

The early church was growing exponentially, but what accompanied that growth was the need to minister to more and more people. Peter and the disciples were focused upon spreading the gospel and working within the gifts God had entrusted to them. However, when criticism arose from the Hellenists (Jews who grew up outside of Israel and had embraced Greek culture) regarding providing for the widows, the disciples called a meeting (Acts 6).

The disciples were in agreement that the widows needed to be cared for, but who was to oversee that ministry? They decided to appoint seven men of good reputation who were full of the Holy Spirit and wisdom to give help and support to their widows. This was a sensible decision; not because the disciples did not want to wait on the widows, but rather so they could be available to focus on spreading the gospel. It is likely the disciples were keenly aware of the brevity of their time on the earth. For them to oversee the administration of provisions to the widows, it would mean halting the work of fulfilling the Great Commission which did not seem to be the best use of their time or talents.

After the seven men were chosen, the disciples prayed and laid hands on them, commissioning them to go forward and serve the Lord. The result was a success. Acts 6:7 records the outcome of this well-made decision, "Then the word of God spread and the number of disciples multiplied greatly in Jerusalem, and a great many of the priests were obedient to the faith."

There are some practical lessons from this story. First, we need to recognize our gifts. God has given all of us, as His children, gifts to use for Him. It is our job to know them and then put them to good use. Second, we should be aware of our time. There are 1,440 minutes in a day. How are we putting that time to use for the Lord? Many "good" and "worthwhile" opportunities are available to serve. We must pray and seek the Lord to know not only which ones are within our gifting, but where does God want us assisting?

The first 11 verses of 1 Peter 4 are overflowing with wisdom. As you read the text, may the Lord speak directly into your life and the areas He has you serving for Him. The clock is ticking; let's be good stewards of our time and invest it well.

RECEIVING God's Word

Open in Prayer

Read 1 Peter 4:1-11

EXPERIENCING God's Word

Experience 1: 1 Peter 4:1-9

1. Read 1 Peter 4:1. Chapter 4 begins with the word "therefore." Peter is still building upon the foundation he laid for us in Chapter 3 that sin was paid for by Jesus' death on the cross once and for all. Jesus was fully man and fully God, yet He had to suffer as a man without using His power as part of the Godhead. Why is it a comfort to know Jesus suffered in the flesh? What is the mind we are told to arm ourselves with? Think back to 1 Peter 3:8 for additional support.

   a. Read Hebrews 4:14-16. What does this verse tell you about Jesus as both man and God? How is this an encouragement as we face suffering and temptation?

2. The last part of verse 1 suggests a particular action we need to choose. What is it, and why is it critical for personal holiness?

3. We are all given a set amount of time on this earth. According to verse 2, how should the believer be living?

4. Read 1 Peter 4:3. List the ways someone, prior to knowing Christ as their Lord and Savior, might have chosen to spend their time?

   a. This is an opinion question and one just for you to consider. Why do you think Peter referred to life before Christ as a "lifetime?"

5. In verse 4 who is "they" referring to, and what three things do these people do and think? Explain.

> "Flood of dissipation" - this word "dissipation" in the Greek is "anachysis" which means a pouring out or an overflow. Metaphorically this means the excess or flood of riot in which a dissolute life pours forth." (Blueletterbible.com, Greek lexicon)

6. Read 1 Peter 4:5. What is the warning found in this verse?

    a. Read Psalm 9:8. What type of a judge is God, and how does He judge?

    b. Read John 5:24. How do we escape the penalty for our sin that would result in eternal separation from God?

c. Read Revelation 20:11-15. What do these verses say regarding the last judgement?

7. Read 1 Peter 4:6. Why is it so vital for believers to live and speak a life that glorifies God?

a. Read Colossians 3:5-10, 12-17. Make a list of those things a child of God should put off and then make a list of those thing we should put on.

8. In 1 Peter 4:7 what does Peter mean when he says," the end of all things is at hand?" What are the "all things?"

9. Read 1 Peter 4:7-9. In light of the "end of all things," as followers of Jesus, how are we commanded to live? Why is this an example to those who do not follow Christ?

a. Why does Peter say, "above all things...put on love" in verse 8? Read Proverbs 10:12 and note the contrast in this proverb.

b. Read 1 Corinthians 13:4-8a. How is love defined, and based on this, why does Peter tell us that above all the things we can do we need to have love for one another?

Experience 2: 1 Peter 4:10-11

1. Read 1 Peter 4:10-11. What have we all received, and what are we to do with it?

2. Read the following verses and fill in the chart below with the gifts described in the passage.

Romans 12:3-8	1 Corinthians 12: 4-11 and 27-31	Ephesians 4:11-13
1.	1.	1.
2.	2.	2.
3.	3.	3.
4.	4.	4.
5.	5.	5.
6.	6.	
7.	7.	
	8.	
	9.	
	10.	
	11.	
	12.	
	13.	

3. Many people mistakenly say, "I don't have a gift," or "I'm ill-equipped to use the gift I was given." How does 1 Peter 4:10 speak truth into those false statements?

a. When exercising your spiritual gift(s), who should receive all glory, accolades, and attention?

A ACTING on God's Word

"...that he no longer should live the rest of his *time* in the flesh for the lusts of men, but for the will of God. For we have spent enough of our past *lifetime* in doing the will of the Gentiles – when we walked in lewdness, lusts, drunkenness, revelries, drinking parties, and abominable idolatries."

1 Peter 4:2-3

I (Stacy) can't help but read these verses with a heavy heart. I was saved at the age of 6, raised by a mother who loved Jesus, albeit rather legalistically, and instructed me in the truths of God's Word; however, for years into adulthood I struggled to live a life that pleased God. For the believer who chooses sin, I believe there is a constant tension that exists in our hearts; we desire the things of God, but instead we choose to walk according to our selfish desires and lusts. I wanted Jesus and the world. The two can't co-exist. But, oh how I tried. From high school and into college, I chose the world. If my life's movie real was on rewind and you saw me during those years, you would not say, "Now there's a girl who lives for Jesus." I am ashamed to say I spent my time doing many of the things described in these verses.

Enough of my past lifetime was wasted on things of no eternal value. By God's grace, He pursued me by using some difficult life circumstances to get at the deep sins of my heart. I recommitted my life to Christ at the age of 22, but it wasn't until around 2002 that I believe I fully surrendered my whole heart to His authority. I didn't want to live this life for me. It wasn't fun nor was it fulfilling. It left me empty and worn out. I wanted to live for God.

These verses hit close to home. Maybe they do for you too? These verses speak of the time God has given us and asks us what we are doing with it.

1. Time. Our verses speak of the time we have been given. I counted six different references to time in these verses. We have a set lifespan determined by God. We have 365 days every year and 24 hours in each day. We can fall into the trap of thinking time is our own. Would you agree with this statement? Why or why not?

2. Describe your "past lifetime" before you were saved or fully surrendered your heart to the Lord. What things characterized your priorities and how you spent your time?

3. When did the Lord get ahold of your heart, and when did you see changes in the ways you spent your free time, your entertainment choices, or the people you chose to spend time with? Describe these changes.

4. In 1 Peter 4:4 Peter tells us people will take notice of these changes too and will not be so thrilled with them. They may even speak evil of you. Have you experienced this? Explain if you have.

5. Peter tells us in 1 Peter 4:7 we are to be serious and watchful in our prayers. With time in mind, why is there (or should there be) such brevity to this command as a believer? Does your life and prayer life communicate this brevity?

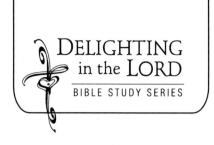

6. Above all, God desires that we use the life He gave us for His glory and His purposes. Our lives will and should look different from many of those around us. Are there specific situations you encounter where "different" produces tension or a struggle? Why? Can you identify the root cause of this struggle?

a. What things can you do or how might your perspective need to change so the next time you encounter this situation you don't make it about you, but God is glorified?

 **DELIGHTING** in God's Word

Looking back at our verses, how has the Lord prompted you to pray?

Write a verse from the lesson God has spoken to your heart.

Close in Prayer

"The one thing I ask of the Lord - the thing I seek most - is to live in the house of the Lord all the days of my life, delighting in the Lord's perfections and meditating in his temple." Psalm 27:4

DELIGHTING
in the LORD
BIBLE STUDY SERIES

WEEK 9

THE FIERY TRIAL

1 Peter 4:12-19

So much was happening at a rapid speed as Peter stopped to take in the moment. He was a changed man now filled with the Holy Spirit, surrendered to Christ, and overflowing with an inexpressible joy. Peter couldn't help but replay the previous day's events in his mind. It was God who gave him the words to speak to the thousands gathered in Jerusalem to celebrate Pentecost; God who spoke through Him and God who saved over 3,000 people. What rejoicing took place that day and the days that followed as new believers gathered together, opened the Holy Scriptures, prayed, and praised God for the new life in Christ they were enjoying.

His thoughts were quickly interrupted with the awareness of the time. He needed to get to the temple for afternoon prayer. He met up with John, and as 3 p.m. quickly approached, the two made their way to the temple gate called Beautiful. Stepping into the gate, a man called for their attention. Peter had seen him there before. Each day this lame man sat at the gate while begging for handouts; anything to help him. Peter's heart was moved. This man needed Jesus. His physical state was one of brokenness since birth; his spiritual state was no different. Fixing his eyes on this man, Peter called for his attention, "Look at us" (Acts 3:4). Expectantly, the man looked with his hand outstretched. Peter had a gift to give, but it wasn't silver or gold. In the name of Jesus, Peter instructed the lame man to rise up and walk. Reaching out his hand, Peter pulled him to his feet. The movement in the temple court stopped. Voices hushed as people watched with curiosity. The man's excitement broke through the silence as he leaped, praising and glorifying God. Holding onto Peter and John, he entered the temple court with them as they made their way to Solomon's Porch. Many followed closely behind.

Peter took the opportunity to tell them about Jesus. With boldness and conviction, Peter shared the gospel once again. By this time, word had gotten to the captain of the temple, the priests, and the Sadducees about Peter and John. Making their way to Solomon's Porch, they heard Peter preaching in the name of Jesus and speaking of the resurrection of the dead. They had to shut them up. At once, they arrested Peter and John and placed them in custody. But the gospel message had gone out. God's work had been accomplished as the crowd's hearts were pricked by the very things Peter shared. Thousands put their faith in Jesus that day.

The next day Peter and John were brought to a large gathering of political and religious officials. Undaunted by the crowd and filled with the Holy Spirit, Peter once again spoke of Jesus as the only name by which man can be saved. Looking out in the crowd, Peter saw the lame man from the previous day standing among those gathered. The Jewish leaders marveled at what was being spoken. They, too, saw the healed lame man and could not speak against what had been done. Commanding Peter and John to never speak or teach in the name of Jesus, the rulers decided to let them go. But Peter spoke again saying, "We cannot but speak the things which we have seen and heard" (Acts 4:20). Further threats were given, and Peter and John were released.

Fiery trials and suffering. They come in many forms. For Peter and John, it came this day through threats and imprisonment. Their freedom taken and their convictions challenged as a fiery trial came upon them. Yet, their faith unhindered and their message undeterred, their attitudes were seemingly filled with joy. Jesus had warned his disciples before his death that in order to be His disciples, they must "daily take up their cross, deny themselves and follow after Jesus" (Luke 9:23). Suffering is part of the Christian life. As Jesus suffered, so must we. But it was through Jesus' suffering that people were brought to God. Suffering has purpose. Peter saw this firsthand that day. As many came to Christ, God was glorified and Peter's faith was strengthened. It is this very truth of the Christian faith that Peter addresses in the verses we will study.

I, Stacy, have walked through much suffering and fiery trials over the years. Through some very difficult trials I have learned they all have purpose; purpose for me, purpose for those around me, and most importantly, purpose in God's kingdom. Whatever you may be walking through today, trust God has allowed this trial, and God wants to use this trial in your life to bring you and those around you closer to Him. Just like with Peter, His glory is being revealed through you as you faithfully walk.

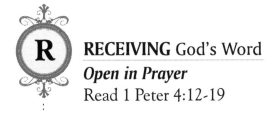

RECEIVING God's Word
Open in Prayer
Read 1 Peter 4:12-19

 **E** **EXPERIENCING** God's Word

1. Read 1 Peter 4:12. How does this verse begin? Why might this stand out concerning the subject manner?

2. In verse 12 Peter says we, as believers, should expect something. What is it, and why is it necessary?

   a. Trials are sometimes hard for us to bear as well as understand. Let's look at why God allows trials in our lives. Read John 9:1-3 and fill in the blanks below.

   This fiery trial was allowed so that the _____ of _____ should be revealed in him. This was not due to a sin issue.

b. Read Hebrews 12:7-11. Fill in the blanks below.

This fiery trial was allowed due to _____. A consequence was necessary. God allows this consequence, or fiery trial, so we become _____ of His _____. God wants to use the trial to yield "_____ fruit of _____ to those who have been trained by it."

c. Read James 1:2-4. Fill in the blanks below.

This fiery trial was allowed in order to _____ your _____.

d. Read Job 42:1-6. Fill in the blank below.

Job suffered loss of life, loss of possession, loss of relationships and loss of health. At the end of verse 5 Job declared to God what these trials produced in him. The fiery trial was allowed so that Job would _____ God more fully.

3. In 1 Peter 4:13 Peter is suggesting we react to suffering in a way contrary to our human nature. How does he describe the way we should react when we experience trials?

a. Suffering allows us to closely identify with Jesus' sufferings. Explain why this is a cause for rejoicing.

b. Read Philippians 3:1 & 3:7-11. Explain Paul's reasons for how joy is possible through suffering.

> "Peter once told Jesus to avoid the suffering of the cross (Mark 8:32-33). Once it seemed strange to the Apostle Peter that his Master should think of suffering. Now he thinks it strange that he could have imagined anything else." (Meyer from David Guzik commentary, Enduring Word)

4. In 1 Peter 4:14 Peter tells us we are blessed when others shame us for our faith in Christ. How are we blessed?

a. From this verse, how does God see the one who shamed or reproached you, and how does God see you, the faithful?

b. Read Matthew 5:10-12. How is rejoicing possible when we are reviled or persecuted for our faith in Christ?

5. Read 1 Peter 4:15. We already learned suffering can come as a consequence to sin. How does this verse address our personal responsibilities so we don't bring suffering upon ourselves?

6. In question 2 of this lesson, we learned from John 9 that suffering can be allowed by God in order to display His glory to others. If our suffering is for the glory of God, what should our reaction look like?

7. In verses 17 and 18 God's judgment begins with His people. His judgment against the person who dies without putting their trust in God will happen at the judgment seat of Christ. Their eternity is one of fire. The believer's eternity is one of blessing. From this verse, how is suffering a form of judgment for God's people now?

"Now is our time of fiery trial (1 Peter 4:12); the ungodly will have their fire later. The fire we endure now purifies us; the fire the ungodly will endure will punish them. Yet we always remember that there is never any punishment from God for us in our sufferings, only purification. For the Christian, the issue of punishment was settled once and for all at the cross, where Jesus endured all the punishment the Christian could ever face from God." (David Guzik commentary, Enduring Word)

8. Read 1 Peter 4:19. How is God described? How does this truth help us commit our souls to Him in the midst of suffering?

 ## ACTING on God's Word

In the front of my Bible, I (Brenda) have a series of statements listed there about how I should see myself before the Lord, my purpose, and my attitude towards ministry. One of the statements says, "May I not be surprised by hardships." I remember writing that particular statement because far too many times trials have blindsided me. I wasn't expecting them; in fact, I used to think because I served the Lord, I should be spared some hardships and be given an easier road.

Peter tells us, "Beloved, do not think it strange concerning the fiery trial which is to try you, as though some strange thing happened to you; but rejoice to the extent that you partake of Christ's sufferings, that when His glory is revealed, you may also be glad with exceeding joy" (1 Peter 4:12-13). Peter is reminding us not to think that trials and suffering are strange, but rather to anticipate them and rejoice when we experience them! No one I know is signing up for fiery trials or suffering, yet we learned there are benefits to the trials we endure. Joy can be experienced when our attitude and perspective on suffering is focused on Christ rather than ourselves.

1. When a fiery trial starts, do you question if God is angry with you, and therefore, the trial is a punishment?

    a. Or have you ever thought that if you could just be refined enough, somehow the suffering would stop? If so, why?

    b. What did you learn this week that would correct this misperception for the purposes of trials?

2. Have you ever considered reversing your thinking about suffering from, "Why me God?" to "Why not me God?" What did you learn this week from our lesson that would help you make this shift in thinking?

3. When we suffer, we can be drawn closer to the Lord because we are partaking in a deeper understanding of His suffering for us. In what ways have you understood this truth in times of trial? How did the text refresh your memory on this topic?

4. The pain in a trial often makes us focus on ourselves. What if, instead of looking at ourselves, we turned our focus toward eternity? If we contemplated the fact that our trials on this earth are both temporary and the worst we will ever endure, how could this change our attitude and make us more joy filled?

D DELIGHTING in God's Word

Looking back at our verses, how has the Lord prompted you to pray?

Write a verse from the lesson God has spoken to your heart.

Close in Prayer

DELIGHTING
in the LORD
BIBLE STUDY SERIES

WEEK 10

STAND STRONG

1 Peter 5

Evening was falling across the Sea of Galilee when Jesus instructed His disciples to get into a boat and sail across to Capernaum. He sent them on ahead so He could be alone to pray. Obediently, the men began to head toward their destination.

The Sea of Galilee was a body of water Peter knew well because he had spent much of his life making a living by catching fish from its waters. The trip to Capernaum should have been simply traveling from one shore to another, but three miles into their voyage, a storm kicked up. Being very familiar with storms coming out of nowhere on the Sea of Galilee, Peter was likely alarmed by the whitecaps forming on the lake. However, what scared him perhaps even more was the man walking on the water and heading towards him. Having never seen anything like this in his life, Peter concluded he had encountered a ghost. Fear gripped Peter's heart, but the voice of Jesus called out saying, "Be of good cheer! It is I; do not be afraid."

Although Thomas is normally the disciple notoriously known for doubting, in this moment Peter is also a doubter. He says to Jesus, "Lord, if it is you, command me to come to You on the water," and Jesus answered Peter by saying, "Come." But his doubt transformed into trust when Peter got out of the boat and stepped onto the water. However, somewhere between step one and reaching Jesus, the reality of what he was doing struck him. Standing on water with winds whipping around him, Peter began to look around, doubted he could continue, and just like that his faith dissipated and fear replaced faith. He cried out, "Lord, save me!" Immediately Jesus put His hand out to Peter and held him securely. Jesus, perhaps with a gentle smile and love in His eyes, looked at His impetuous disciple and said, "O you of little faith, why did you doubt?" With that, together they climbed back into the boat.

Maybe this very experience was in the back of Peter's mind as he wrote 1 Peter 5. Just as the storm brewed on the Sea of Galilee the night he walked with Jesus on the water, storms were buffeting the lives of the early Christians. Fear had gripped Peter's heart as he began to sink into the Sea of Galilee, and likely fear was robbing the New Testament believers of their peace as they faced severe persecution.

But just as Jesus had kept Peter from sinking, Jesus would keep the early church as well. He would be their strength in weakness. He would carry them across stormy trials the enemy was using to buffet them.

Perhaps you are facing circumstances that require faith you have never been able to exhibit in the past. Is Jesus saying to you, "Be full of faith and do not doubt; I'm bringing you to a new level of trust with Me?" As you submit your life into His care, He will show you things you never thought possible. Come to Him humbly, full of faith, and you will overcome your storm and stand strong. May the words of Peter be a great reminder of what Jesus promises His children as we combat the enemy and trust Him with the suffering He allows.

RECEIVING God's Word

Open in Prayer
Read 1 Peter 5:1-14

EXPERIENCING God's Word

Experience 1: 1 Peter 5:1-4

1. In verse 1 how does Peter describe himself, and who is he speaking to specifically in the first four verses?

2. How does Peter describe the responsibilities of an elder in verses 2-3?

a. What adjectives does Peter use to describe the way by which they carry out their responsibilities?

3. In verse 4 who is the Chief Shepherd, and what reward is given to believers at His coming?

Experience 2: 1 Peter 5:5-7

1. Read 1 Peter 5:5. Peter addresses a different group of people. Who are they?

a. What does he command them to do in verse 5a, and why is this important?

b. Peter now includes all his readers in this same exhortation. Why does he add humility to the exhortation? How are the two exhortations linked together?

c. Peter quotes Proverbs 3:34. Here pride and humility are contrasted based on God's response to these attitudes. How does God view each one?

d. Bible scholar and commentator Matthew Henry said, "Humility is the great preserver of peace and order in all Christian churches and society; consequently pride is the great disturber." Explain this statement.

2. Read Philippians 2:3-10. Jesus is our ultimate example of humility. Write down what you learn from Him on this topic.

3. Read 1 Peter 5:6-7. The verse starts with the word *"therefore,"* so Peter's next command hinges on what was previously said in verse 5 concerning God's heart on pride and humility. What does it mean to humble yourself under God's hand?

Week 10: Stand Strong

a. How does God give grace to the believer when they humble themselves under God's hand?

4. Read 1 Peter 5:7. What are we encouraged to do in this verse?

a. Why should we do this?

b. How does doing this demonstrate humility and submission?

Experience 3: 1 Peter 5:8-11

1. In the verses above we learned God cares for us and wants to help us. Read 1 Peter 5:8. We are introduced to the one who is against us. Describe him and explain what he desires to do to the believer.

2. Having seen the enemy at work in not only his life but also in the lives of those around him, Peter starts verse 8 with two strong commands. List them and define them in your own words.

3. Let's learn a bit more about the adversary. Look up the following verses and note what you learn about him.

John 8:44

John 10:10

Matthew 4:1

a. The enemy has a future, and it is not a good one. Read Revelation 20:7-10 and describe what his future holds.

4. You have just familiarized yourself with your enemy. Based upon what you read, it's clear you are at war with him daily. Read 1 Peter 5:9. Fill in the following phrases with Peter's suggestions to fight the enemy.

_____ him,

(stand) _____ in the faith.

_____ that the same sufferings are experienced (by others around the world)

5. Read Ephesians 6:10-18. In a war you need the right protection. We are in a spiritual war every day. From these verses, describe the armor that God gives us and desires us to use.

    a. In Ephesians 6:10-18 there is a word that is repeated multiple times. What is this word, and why is this significant in battle?

    b. Finally, we are unable to do anything without the power of Christ. Read 1 John 4:4 and explain how the Holy Spirit in you gives you victory over the enemy.

6. Read 1 Peter 5:10-11. Peter takes his readers back to the topic of suffering once again because it is the main theme of the entire book. No one is immune to suffering. In the midst of suffering, God is always at work even if we don't see it or feel it at the time. However, Peter reminds us throughout the whole book that there is an encouraging progression which can happen when we yield to the Lord and His will through times of suffering. Complete the list below based on verses 10-11.

- We have a living hope (1 Peter 1:3)

- Be holy (1 Peter 1:15)

- Obey the truth (1 Peter 1:22)

- Be of one mind (1 Peter 3:8)

- Sanctify the Lord in your heart (1 Peter 3:15)

- Be serious and watchful in your prayers (1 Peter 4:7)

- Have fervent love for one another (1 Peter 4:8)

- Be submissive (1 Peter 5:5)

- Be humble (1 Peter 5:6)

- Be sober and vigilant (1 Peter 5:8)

- Be steadfast in the faith (1 Peter 5:9)

- You will be _____ (1 Peter 5:10)

- You will be _____ (1 Peter 5:10)

- You will be _____ (1 Peter 5:10)

- You will be _____ (1 Peter 5:10)

- Who receives the glory in and through all of this? _____
  (1 Peter 5:11)

Experience 4: 1 Peter 5:12-14

1. As Peter wraps up his letter, he mentions Silvanus (Silas) who has been a faithful brother to him and to others. Read 1 Peter 5:12. Peter writes a powerful statement. What is it, and why might he include this in his closing remarks?

2. Read 1 Peter 5:13-14. Peter ends with such tenderness by mentioning the church in Rome which is referred to as Babylon and John Mark who is like a spiritual son. From the moment Peter was called to be a disciple, his life was shaped by Christ. As he closes, perhaps he recalled his encounter with the resurrected Lord in John 20:19-29. Read this account and notice the similarities found between the text in John and the text in 1 Peter. What is the final encouragement Peter is giving us?

A ACTING on God's Word

This past year, my (Stacy) second son, Seth, left for college. God's plan took him much farther from home than I would have chosen. Seth is a freshman at Wheaton College located just outside Chicago. Now my two oldest boys are in Illinois and Indiana. There aren't many weekend visits or quick trips to see them. I'm quite thankful for the way various technologies (cell phones, Skype on my computer, etc.) make staying in touch easier. Yet, I am keenly aware they are on their own 24/7, making their own choices and dealing with their own sets of struggles without me. For 18 years I stood on the front lines with them by giving them advice, praying with them, instructing them in God's Word, and helping them work through difficulties. Above all, I helped them stand strong in the Lord.

When we dropped Seth off on the Wheaton campus this past August, Barclay and I each gave him a letter when we said our good-byes. My letter was not only a love note to my son, but it also offered encouragement and exhortation; it was a reminder about how to stand strong in challenges and how to stand strong in the Lord.

This week we are finishing up the book of 1 Peter. It was a letter from the heart of an overseer and teacher in the church to his precious and beloved brothers and sisters in Christ. Peter's life is drawing to a close, and he knew he might never see these people again on this side of eternity. He had love and encouragement to share with them from the vantage point of walking with Jesus, being an eye witness to Christ's suffering and resurrection, and then being used powerfully as God's witness. Peter experienced suffering and blessing, warfare and victory, and learned from walking with Jesus what Jesus offered for this life and the next.

Week 10: Stand Strong

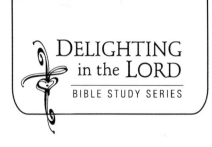

1. In the questions from this week's lesson, we gave you a list of exhortations from Peter throughout his letter. These exhortations were written not only for life in general, but also for encouragement in trials and difficulties. Every one of us is going through something right now that is challenging us. It might be a relationship, a physical ailment, a spiritual battle, or it could be a physical trial of some sort. But there is something God is using to work in your life. What is your greatest struggle right now?

a. Using this list below, next to each command/exhortation write how you can apply this principle to your current situation identified above. In those areas where you might not be obedient right now, pause and confess this sin to the Lord and ask Him to help you in this area.

- We have a living hope (1 Peter 1:3)

- Be holy (1 Peter 1:15)

- Obey the truth (1 Peter 1:22)

- Be of one mind (1 Peter 3:8)

- Sanctify the Lord in your heart (1 Peter 3:15)

- Be serious and watchful in your prayers (1 Peter 4:7)

- Have fervent love for one another (1 Peter 4:8)

- Be submissive (1 Peter 5:5)

- Be humble (1 Peter 5:6)

- Be sober and vigilant (1 Peter 5:8)

- Be steadfast in the faith (1 Peter 5:9)

b. Now write a letter to yourself as you would write a letter to a loved one who is going through your current struggle. Instruct yourself in godly principles and offer encouragement and godly truths. Sometimes it is easier for us to help others than to humble ourselves under God and allow Him to help us.

c. Next, write a letter to a child, grandchild, or friend. Write the letter as Peter has written this letter to us. May the letter be one of encouragement as you remind a loved one of the things of God. If God so directs, give that letter to the loved one.

2. Finally, look back through the study questions of 1 Peter.

   a. What stood out to you the most?

   b. What part of your walk has God been working on since the start of this study? What progress have you seen Him make as you've submitted to His authority over you in this area?

   c. How would you summarize the book of 1 Peter in one or two sentences?

D DELIGHTING in God's Word

Looking back at our verses, how has the Lord prompted you to pray?

Write a verse from the lesson God has spoken to your heart.

Close in Prayer

BIBLIOGRAPHY

Guzik, David. *"The Enduring Word Bible Commentary."* Enduring Word, enduringword.com.

Ironside, H.A. *James and 1 and 2 Peter: An Ironside Expository Commentaries.* Loizeaux Brothers, 1994.

Radmacher, Earl D., et al. *The NKJV Study Bible.* New King James Version. 2nd ed., Thomas Nelson, 2007.

Stibbs, Alan M. T*he First Epistle General of Peter.* Inter-Varsity Press, 1983.

Walls, David R., and Max E. Anders. *I & II Peter, I, II & III John, Jude.* Holman Reference, 1999.

Walvoord, John F., and Roy B. Zuck. *Bible Knowledge Commentary.* David C. Cook, 1983.

Wiersbe, Warren W. *Be Hopeful (1 Peter): How to Make the Best of Times Out of Your Worst of Times.* David C. Cook, 1982.

www.blueletterbible.com

Made in the USA
Middletown, DE
30 September 2020